SANTANDER

Rambling on Borrowed Time

David Ellison

For Mom and Dad

And for Michael,
my student,
whom Life cheated, then abandoned.
For all the Michaels.

"Caminante, son tus huellas
el camino y nada más;
Caminante, no hay camino,
se hace camino al andar."

ANTONIO MACHADO

CONTENTS

PREFACE

In 1981, fresh out of college, I ventured out to discover the world and myself.

While waiting for an overnight ferry to carry me from England to Ireland, I strolled at sunset atop a bluff overlooking the Celtic Sea. I watched a small, white gull, golden with twilight, hover wind-wavering just a few meters above me. To my surprise and delight, the gull followed me as I continued along the path.

Was he an omen? The Holy Spirit assuring me that I would never really travel alone? (I was quite religious at the time.) Or just a simple bird joining me in savoring the beauty and wonder of the moment?

It was an auspicious beginning to a nearly two-year odyssey, my first of many. The adventure would lead me to the depths of a small café in rain-drenched Santiago de Compastela, Spain, where I doubted my journey and myself completely; to the heights of a frozen ridge in Los Picos de Europa, where, with ice axe, crampons, and intrepid new-found friends, I climbed my first breathtaking summit; to a small, after-hours English language school on the Iberian Peninsula's northern coast (Santander) where, unwittingly, I fell in love with teaching; to so many unimagined places, people, and discoveries which subtly, profoundly, marked me forever.

Nonetheless, it's the mystical moment with the gull I've treasured most; and I wonder if it will be the final memory I'll let slip just before I breathe my last. It defined me, instilling a deep-seated, unquenchable longing to ever be on the precipice of yet another adventure.

Even now, when driving to school on what could be just one more mundane morning, I often sing the same words I did during that first, glorious gallivant so long ago, the song an anxious Maria sang in *The Sound of Music*, just before her foray into the wide world: "What will this day be like? I wonder. What will my future be? It could be so exciting, to be out in the world, to be free!"

The song reminds me that each day can be a journey, perhaps even an adventure, especially in the life of a teacher. After all, my students never fail to surprise me (or to make me laugh).

I see so much of myself in these children. Most long to venture out someday to discover the world and themselves. Oh, if only I can keep such a precious spirit alive—in their hearts as well as mine.

What follows is a loosely organized chronicle of other such rambles, the memories and musings I've gleaned from a half-century of rambling about life, schools, and the world. I wrote most of them piecemeal over eighteen years for *The Argus* and *The Daily Review* (Bay Area News Group).

But, where to start? Maria knew: "Let's start at the very beginning, a very good place to start." So, I'll start long before I met that mysterious gull high on a British cliff. I'll start with another
auspicious beginning, my traumatic birth...

PART ONE: RAMBLING ABOUT LIFE

"Life is either a daring adventure...or nothing."

HELEN KELLER

THE GIFT

A month before I was supposed to be born, my umbilical cord ruptured, sending my mom and me to the hospital, bleeding profusely. "There's no hope for your baby," the doctor informed my distraught dad, "and you better pray for your wife."

Dad drove my three older siblings to Saint Margaret Mary's Church near Cleveland, Ohio, told them to kneel at the altar and to pray like they'd never prayed before. When they asked what for, he replied, frantic, "Just pray!"

I was born by emergency caesarian section. The doctor at the Catholic hospital took one look at me and baptized me on the spot, certain I would soon perish. A few minutes later, a nurse repeated the sacrament for the same reason. (Counting my formal baptism back at Saint Mary's afterward, I've been baptized three times.)

When my mom woke up, groggy from blood-loss and anesthesia, she asked the nurse, hoping against hope, "How is my baby?"

"It was a boy."

My mom collapsed back onto the pillow and grieved. "It WAS a boy," she heard, assuming the nurse had put my death as tenderly as possible.

And on the third day (intone that with sanctimonious melodrama, please), the family pediatrician visited my mom.

"What are you doing here?" she asked in despair.

"I've come to see your baby."

"My baby's dead!"

"No he's not!" The pediatrician hurried out and returned a few moments later with the miracle baby, me, incubator and all. "He's doing just fine!"

My resurrection is now the stuff of legend in the Ellison family, recounted countless times at reunions. Its telling includes how angry my mom later became with her brother, Jerry. When she'd proudly unwrapped my blankets to show me off, he'd burst out laughing, "Gosh, when we get 'em that small, we throw 'em back!"

After one such retelling, my mom whispered to me—half in jest and half in earnest—the same advice she'd given my brother, Tim, who'd also once flirted with death: "You know, if I were you, I'd be worried. God's kept you alive for something."

Unlike my mom, however, I've long doubted Providence. (Apparently, even three baptisms weren't enough to make my faith stick.) If, however, it turns out that there has been a Divine plan for my life, I suspect my teaching and my writing have been essential to my purpose on Earth.

One thing is for sure: I am fortunate to be alive, living on borrowed time. (Attending the funerals of some of my young students has driven that realization home poignantly.)

And so, I've felt a special responsibility to live this life well. I used to repeat to myself that wonderful but severe adage, "Live every day as if it were your last. One of these days you'll be right."

I've since modified it to my own liking: "Live every day as if it were a gift. And every day you'll be right."

Let me savor that gift, and make good use of it.

A TALE OF TWO TEACHERS

It was 1973, and I was an 8th grader at a parochial school outside Cleveland. I suffered that year. My classmates were a rough bunch, treating teachers and each other with a very unchristian-like cruelty. In fact, they'd convinced two teachers to quit midyear.

Had the option been available to me, I would have fled as well. The exiled teachers were the lucky ones.

My worst hour of the day was gym class. I was a runt of a kid— puny, scrawny, shy, always picked on, always picked last. I cowered in the corner during dodge ball games.

If only the teacher had nurtured my latent athletic ability! (I would discover it only many years later, after college.) But no, he treated me with withering disdain since I wasn't on the football team. Worse, he threatened students with a large bamboo pole, and made kids cry each time he used it. He terrified me.

One day when the bell ending gym class had finally rung, I let out a whoop of joy.

Nonplussed, the teacher ordered me to his office. There was no bamboo pole for me, however. "So, Ellison, you like to scream, do you? Well, then, start screaming!" He made me stand there like an idiot in his office, shrieking again and again, while my classmates filed by the open door, laughing.

I still despise that man, even though I forgot his name ages ago.

I'll never forget Sister Mary Rita Lynn, though. She hadn't received the memo about the 8th grade hellions. She had fun with us. She liked us. Why, she even liked me!

One day, Sister taught us to write poems in response to a movie we'd seen about various exotic (to us in the Midwest) sports. She helped us brainstorm sensory images, which she listed on the board, then asked us to arrange them in new, creative ways. "Poetry is easy, kids! I can't wait to see what you create."

I knew I had no talent, but I tried anyway. (I'd do anything for Sister Rita Lynn.) Twenty minutes later, I showed her my verses about a surfer engaged in a fierce battle with the waves. "And only the end will tell," I concluded, "who is master of who." (Sister made me change the final "who" to "whom," giving me a quick mini-lesson on subjective versus objective pronouns.)

The next class was history with another teacher whose name I've forgotten; and in the middle of some interminable lecture, a messenger came from Sister: Could she please have Dave Ellison's draft poem about the surfer to use as a model for the other class?

Numb, I took it out of my binder and handed it over. I sat dumbfounded for the remainder of the period, awed by the fact that, at that moment, Sister was reading my poem aloud to other students, praising it—praising me.

How much of my writing today do I owe to that wonderful woman? My battered self-esteem survived because of her.

In 1973, one teacher humiliated me. Another resurrected me. Such is the awful, awesome power of a teacher. I vow that, like Sister Mary Rita Lynn, I will use mine to enable my students to recognize their talent and their goodness.

And I pray they remember my name.

THE VEST

I thought a vest would transform me.

When I was a high school sophomore, I'd resigned myself to never fitting in or being popular, much less respected. My freshman nickname, Squeaky, had stuck to me even though my pubescent voice had finally settled. I tried to pretend I didn't mind the constant ridicule, but I did.

It was only natural that I'd look up to my counter-culture older brother, Tim. A senior, he, too, fit into no school social group, but not because he couldn't. No, Tim beat his own path through life.

Oh, how I wanted be a maverick like him, instead of a nobody!

The greatest symbol of Tim's courageous independence, at least as I saw it, was his tan, leather, cowboy vest, which he wore to school every day. His trademark, the vest had silver stars on each breast with a leather tassel dangling from both of them, as well as a row of other tassels along the back. In a Catholic high school where everyone had to wear a tie, it was totally out of place.

That's why Tim wore the vest. It pushed the edge of decorum, defied the teachers, challenged the status quo.

No one poked fun at Tim because it would have been pointless. He didn't care what anyone thought. I suspect many secretly envied him for his ability to so carelessly do his own thing.

I know I did. So, I asked my mom to give me the same vest for Christmas. I hoped that, when I put it on, I'd don as well Tim's self-confidence, the respect he had because he didn't want it.

As I walked into first period Geometry class, proud as could be, the class burst into pandemonium. Everyone pointed, guffawed, and shook their heads in disbelief and derision. Even the teacher (what was his name?), who tried to calm everyone down with "It's only a vest, kids!" did so with a barely disguised smirk.

I tried to just nonchalantly sit down at my desk amid the uproar, but my scarlet ears betrayed me.

That scene repeated itself in every class. The worst was lunchtime when students from across the cafeteria stood on their chairs to get a glimpse of the buffoon in the cowboy vest.

Now, nearly fifty years later, even though I still wince at the memory, I also laugh at its absurdity. What's more, I respect the humiliated boy I once was. Throughout that horrible day, I never once took the damned vest off. I even stubbornly wore it again the next day, just to show everyone I didn't care what they thought (even though I did).

The third morning, though, I contemplated the vest hanging in the closet, and chose to leave it there. With the first glimmerings of insight and maturity, I knew I'd never be able to wear it comfortably. Only Tim could. It was time for me to find, maybe even make my own path in life, just as he had done.

THE JERK

I lied to Miss O'Donnell. I lied about her. I even convinced myself for a time that I hated her. I was such a jerk!

I'm sure Miss O'Donnell was pleasant enough that first day of my freshman history class. But, as far as I was concerned, she'd committed a mortal sin: She'd insisted, despite the stifling heat, that I button my collar and straighten my tie—as was befitting a proper young man in a Jesuit high school.

Why I made such a fuss I still cannot fathom. But I told all my friends that Miss O'Donnell was a mean, unreasonable, ruthless tyrant.

Of course, the matter of the tie was not enough to substantiate such a review. So, I simply invented terrible stories about her.

It was inevitable that Miss O'Donnell would one day hear of them. On another sweltering day she asked to see me after class. One by one, she recounted every last lie. I stood there, fidgeting, avoiding her eyes, finally speechless. She gave me no lecture or punishment. She simply made me remain there for a few moments of unbearable embarrassment. And then, with an amused smile, she allowed me to slink away.

I wish I could say I'd mended my ways after that. I was a lot more careful with my lies. But I despised Miss O'Donnell more than ever. Indeed, although I could not claim credit for her nickname, "Ann of a Thousand Thighs," I propagated it throughout the school.

The amazing thing was that, despite everything I did, Miss O'Donnell still liked me. Oh, she knew I was a jerk. Even so, she had faith that I would eventually grow up.

Deep down, in spite my professed hatred for her, I knew she liked me. I suppose that's why I tried to make her proud of me in the end. Why else would I have struggled so long on my final project for her?

I finally did grow up, and now a lot of my students are jerks. (Sometimes there is justice in the world!) They lie to me and about me.

They've even invented some terribly cruel—but very amusing—nicknames for me. ("Roll-On," a sinister reference to my bald head, is my favorite.) Sometimes I'd like to scream at them. But then I remember how immature I was, how patient Miss O'Donnell was. Because I remember, I can often overlook my students' silly, sometimes maddening behavior. I like my students anyway.

I have Miss O'Donnell to thank for that. And if the jerks I teach knew about her, they'd thank her too.

HOW TO LIVE

I t's strange that of all the images I cherish of Mr. Murphy, the most vivid is his palsied arm.

The evening was dreary, probably after a late rehearsal, and I had just helped Mr. Murphy into his car so his son could drive him home. Murphy's face was uncharacteristically fatigued, and his right arm hung lifelessly at his side. I had to lift it myself and place it nonchalantly on his lap before slamming the door.

As his car sped away, I felt my first pang of worry, the startling realization that The Great Mr. Murphy—icon, legend, god—was in fact oh so terribly mortal. He died two months later.

I could never pity Mr. Murphy. He made sure of that the first week of Freshman Speech class. He explained matter-of-factly how Polio had struck him as a young man, leaving him captive in his wheelchair, harnessed to a respirator. A few days later, in the middle of one of his lectures, he abruptly disconnected the respirator tube, stood shakily up, and limped to the podium. When he saw our eyes grow wide in astonishment, he feigned surprise. "Oh, didn't you know I could take a short walk?" Then he grinned. The joke was on us. No, no one could pity Mr. Murphy.

Everyone respected him, though. In addition to Speech, he taught Government, and managed all the school's fund raising. But it was his genius as a drama director that made his fame.

Mr. Murphy could deftly manage a pompous choreographer, an emotional music director, an unsteady conductor, and a cast and crew of well over a hundred immature students. He instilled in us all a deep love of the theater. More importantly, he taught us discipline, synergy, and pride. A good amount of my high school education, and virtually all of my growing-up took place after school on his stage.

It wasn't easy for him. Boy, could he lose his temper! All too often he'd defy his respirator and bellow out a "Shuuuuut uuuuuuuup!" loud enough to silence even a hall-full of unruly teenagers.

Nor was I an angel. "Ellison, you're a damn ham," Mr. Murphy would growl, trying to put me in my place. Once he called backstage during a scene change, shrieking over the headphones, "You lose character on stage again and I'll lower the curtain!" He would've, too. I idolized him, but feared him just as much.

My senior year he gave me the lead in the spring musical. Then he beckoned me to his wheelchair. "I know you'll do fine, Dave," he encouraged me. "But don't forget: No one is indispensable. Not you. Not me. The show will go on without us, so we can't get full of ourselves."

I wonder if he knew he'd soon fulfill his own prophecy.

I dedicated all my performances to Mr. Murphy—not just the ones that spring, but all my succeeding roles as an actor and a teacher. I still can't ham it up without thinking of him.

It's not just because he died. In spite of a terrible physical fate, he worked tirelessly, joyfully, always in the service of others. And in doing so, he didn't teach me merely speech or government or drama. Mr. Murphy taught me how to live.

"ISN'T THAT RIGHT?

Father Kirby's photograph appeared on the final page of my high school's newsletter. He still wore the same white lab coat, and seemed on the verge of yet another dissertation on the intricacies of subatomic particles. I quickly scanned the accompanying column for news of his latest accomplishment, only to learn that he had recently passed away.

I hadn't thought of Father Kirby once during the many years since I'd left his high school Physics class. Nonetheless, I had to sit for a long time and sadly reminisce.

I wondered if he'd remembered me. I was the short kid who sat in the first row, just by the door. I fell asleep almost every day. (That's why Kirby sat me in front.) I couldn't help it! No matter which class I had after lunch, I would always nod off for fifteen minutes or so. Every once in a while Kirby would awaken me with a loud, "Isn't that right, Mr. Ellison?" I'd blurt out a confused, "Yes, sir!" Usually, I'd just agreed to something quite absurd, and everyone would laugh. I deserved it.

Kirby probably thought I hated Physics. Actually, it was my favorite class. I had always been bored with math. The equations seemed to have no purpose or practical application. I merely plugged in the numbers mechanically, disinterestedly. Father Kirby taught me to use those apparently meaningless equations to precisely describe the world around me, and even to accurately predict how worlds light years away must behave. I marveled that all the galaxies paid homage to the same mathematical laws. In short, I was fascinated. (At least when I wasn't snoring.) I wish I'd told him so.

I recalled one day when Kirby had supervision duty during lunch. He paced up and down the aisles of tables, oblivious to the din, lost in thought. I watched him make one circuit around the cafeteria, and wondered: What was it like to be a priest, without a family? Was he lonely? Didn't he get tired of conducting the same experiments year after year? What did he do for fun? (Did he ever have fun?) For that one, brief instant, I possessed enough maturity to see Father Kirby as a person. I suddenly realized I liked him. The moment of insight passed fleetingly, though, and I went back to throwing my Jell-O across the table.

On the last day of school, Kirby offered us seniors some sage advice (which we promptly forgot), and wished us all a heartfelt good-bye. Then the final bell rang.

Why didn't we stop to thank him, or at least shake his hand? Instead, with a joyous "Free at last!" we dashed out without so much as a glance in his direction. We left him in that silent classroom, to muse upon our ingratitude, alone.

Now, so many years later, I finally recognized my debt to Father Kirby. But, of course, it was too late for a belated "Thank you." What a shame.

I suppose it's only normal. After all, my students are no different. I can only hope that a few of them will likewise remember me one day. Perhaps there'll even be one who will become a teacher, and honor me, just as I will try to honor Father Kirby: She will carry on.

"Isn't that right, Ms. Fletcher?"

THE TITANIC

"It amazes me just how out of shape some of you youngsters are," the University of Notre Dame swimming coach remarked to the other swimmers in towels, apparently intending me to overhear.

I panted briefly before doggedly turning to finish my final laps by myself. "I'm a runner, not a swimmer," I called back with anger to hide my embarrassment.

I'd reverted in desperation to a slow but steady elementary backstroke in order to complete the requisite twenty laps for the physical education lifesaving class. "Whatever possessed me to sign up for this?" I fumed, frustrated that my spindly arms and legs, fine for distance running, helped me not at all in the water. "And he should talk," I mused bitterly, noting the coach's fleshy breasts hanging down over his paunch. He'd been a great swimmer, once, long ago.

The coach rolled his eyes when, stubborn, I'd returned for the next class. What I lacked in strength and ability, though, I made up for with practice. I learned how to jump into a pool and approach a drowning victim without ever allowing my eyes to fall beneath the surface. Then, just out of the flailing victim's grasp, I'd dive down, swim beneath, and emerge behind. I'd grasp his chin with my right hand, pulling him horizontal; then reach across with my left, commencing the classic cross-chest carry with a modified side-stroke—perfect every time.

That's when everything fell apart. You see, I wasn't buoyant. The truth is, when I swam alone, it was all I could do to keep myself afloat. With a victim in tow, however, I'd sink like a rock, drowning us both. Soon none of the other students in class would allow me to practice "saving" them.

At the course's end, the coach kept me after class. "I don't think I can pass you, son. Your form and technique are excellent. Yet, we both know you couldn't save a duck. Anyway, I've asked the department chair to watch you, and make the decision."

The department chair, a dour-faced impatient man, instructed his class to sit on either side of the pool to watch the spectacle, their legs dangling in the water. Oh, this was a nightmare!

"This guy the one?" he queried, peering down at me over his half-rimmed spectacles. "Well, he's going to need someone to save. How about you?" To my horror, he was glancing at my coach. Why I didn't just turn and run out of there I'll never know.

Nonetheless, my coach dutifully swam out to the center of the pool, and I splashed after, another Titanic out towards an inevitable, legendary disaster.

Then a miracle happened. When I grabbed my coach in the cross-chest carry, I discovered that, with all his fat, he bobbed like a cork. It was like saving a humongous life-preserver! Thus, I could devote all my energy to propulsion; and, sure enough, ever-so-slowly, we inched our way back towards the side of the pool.

When my coach did his obligatory roll in the water, I rolled expertly with him. All of a sudden, my coach began to struggle frantically. (This wasn't part of the drill!)

I remembered, though, a trick one of my classmates had shared in the locker room for dealing with hysterical victims. "Just grab them in a bear hug and let 'em have it 'till they calm down. It's fool-proof!" Well, I reached around my coach, just barely able to grasp the fingers of my other hand, and squeezed the living daylights out of him. After a brief, chaotic struggle, he relaxed, and I finally brought the behemoth of my coach to safety.

Gasping, I looked up at the department chair. With a quizzical glance down at my coach, he asked, "So, what's the problem?"

Cue melodramatic music….

POE

The specter coming down the hall frightened me. Absurdly tall, with a large shock of unkempt, black hair and a deeply lined, forbidding face, he swung his cane relentlessly to and fro in front of him. He seemed a bizarre morphing of an Edgar Allen Poe horror story and an elongated, dreary El Greco painting. However, his gaping, vacuous eyes, which were forever tearing, as if from some terribly somber vision they alone could behold—yes, his eyes were the most unnerving. "Poe" was an apt name for him. Pity the poor undergrad who had him for a professor!

The first day second semester, I gasped silently when Poe entered my humanities seminar and, wiping his sightless eyes, introduced himself as Stephen Rogers, the instructor. By spring break, however, I had a new name for him: "Tiresias," the blind seer, the implacable prophet. It had quickly become obvious that it was I, not he, who was blind.

Patiently, sagely, Tiresias opened my eyes to The Great Books—works by Thucydides, Homer, Dante, Descartes, Kant, Shakespeare, Aquinas, Nietzsche—the "dead white men" now in such disrepute.

I still recall as if it were yesterday his haunting reading of T.S. Eliot's poem "The Wasteland"—"April is the cruelest month, breeding lilacs out of the dead land, mixing memory and desire, stirring dull roots with spring rain...." For the first time, I began to appreciate the tremendous beauty of words and the power of the ideas they conveyed, even though I could still only barely understand them.

I changed my major to the liberal arts. "The arts of symbol-making and symbol-using," Tiresias explained, "the symbols we use to describe and ultimately to create our world, and ourselves." "Pre-Unemployment," my father lamented dryly. But Tiresias won out. He awed me.

Indeed, I was afraid to speak during my first classes with him. Who wouldn't be in the presence of a prodigy who could nonchalantly recite obscure epic poems in five languages?

But, through a persistent mix of cajoling, goading, and easy laughter, Tiresias drew me out, igniting all the passion and curiosity I hadn't even known I possessed. Eventually he couldn't shut me up, and often accused me of throwing "intellectual hand-grenades" in the midst of many class discussions.

Finally, one day it was I who insisted on reading aloud a passage from Plato's "Apology," Socrates' stoic response to the judges who'd sentenced him to die: "Death has caught me, the old man. Evil has caught you, the young. Now, I must suffer my fate, and you must suffer yours...."

"That was very fine, David," Tiresias commented after a pause.

"Thanks, Doc," I responded flippantly. And the nickname stuck.

Doctor Stephen Rogers, alias "Doc," coached me through my final, tortuous 40-page senior essay on *The Psalms*. He engendered within my soul a fierce love of learning, a deep belief in the potential nobility of Man. And he gently nudged me in the direction of "the most honorable of all professions," teaching.

Poe, Tiresias, Doc . . . He was my nightmare, my idol, and in the end my friend. He didn't just teach. He inspired. And that is what education is all about.

MOM AND DAD

Many of the simple truths my mom taught me I pass on to my students.

I remember, for example, one suggestion she made when I was twelve years old and had to choose a saint for my confirmation name. St. Philip? St. James? I couldn't decide.

"Choose St. Peter," Mom said. "He was always screwing up!"

I gave her a hurt look.

"Relax, Dave," she laughed, "and listen. Peter was often vain and selfish. He even lied three times and betrayed Jesus. Nonetheless, Jesus chose him to lead His church. Now, there's a saint you can believe in. St. Peter was human, Dave, just like you. So if he could become a saint, you can too."

I recall that advice every Presidents' Day. My teachers taught me that Washington was perfect: He never told a lie, made fools out of the British, and single-handedly founded our nation. Hail, St. Washington! But who could ever aspire to be as wonderful as he?

Because of my mom, I paint a more human (and more realistic) portrait of Washington for my students. I tell them that, like St. Peter, Washington made a few serious mistakes along the way.

In 1754, Washington was a young, brash surveyor. He was supposed to lead a small detachment into the wilderness and discourage the French from building forts there. Washington arrived too late, though. The French already manned their fort, and vastly outnumbered Washington's force. They sent an ambassador to turn Washington back peaceably.

The ambassador never had a chance. Eager for glory, Washington attacked the ambassador's party and killed everyone. Thus began the French and Indian War, which soon escalated into a world war. Oops!

The French easily captured Washington, and released him only because they couldn't take such a foolish, young man seriously. If only they had known!

About twenty-five years later, Washington was the victor, having defeated the British in the American Revolution. (Thanks, ironically, to the help of the French! It was French strategy, French ships, and French cannons that forced the British to surrender at Yorktown.)

Nonetheless, Washington's officers were not celebrating. They had not been paid. They wanted to march on Philadelphia, disband the Continental Congress, and establish military rule. They would receive their pay, by God!

Only one man could stop them. Washington. He knew that everything they did would set a long-lasting precedent. A military coup would lead the new country down a violent path away from democracy. (The French later took that path.) Washington pleaded with his officers to be patient, to trust him. In the end, they did—not because he was a great general (he wasn't), but because he was simply a great human being whom they respected and loved.

The officers never did receive their pay. But neither did their descendants receive the ugly legacy of military dictatorship. We all owe that—and much, much more—to Washington.

I tell my students Washington is a hero they can believe in. Yes, he really screwed up. But he went on to do great things. So can they, I tell them. Just as Mom told me.

✳ ✳ ✳

My parents had the courage to say "No" when I was growing up. At the time I didn't understand. I pouted. I screamed. I ranted and raved. "I'll be the laughing stock at school!" But they remained firm: "No!"

Buying shoes was never an exciting excursion in the Ellison family because we always got the same style, Dexter "Saddle Shoes." ("Army-surplus clod-stompers," I called them.) Oh, how I longed for a pair of penny-loafers! Then I would be able to strut in style! But, "No!" my mom said. The Dexters were eminently practical, their soles lasting a full year, sometimes two. And that was that. Who ever had parents as unreasonable as mine?

The hand-me-down clothes they gave me weren't any better. I can't describe my humiliation when my teachers would compliment them.

"Why, Dave, I remember that beautiful sweater on your oldest brother, Kevin." Aaargh!

The worst were the trips to the barbershop. As quickly as the barber could switch on his electric razor (no need for scissors or a comb!), most of my hair would be gone. "Hair-cuts are too expensive," dad lamented. "We don't want to have to come back here next month because your hair has already grown out."

Easy for him to say! He didn't have to endure the tauntings I did the next morning: "Peach-Fuz! Watermelon!" Sometimes I imagined I hated my parents.

When I became a teacher, though, I appreciated their stubbornness. I dealt with lots of students whose parents hadn't learned to say "No." The results were alternately comical and sad, and sometimes even frightening.

Many boys simply had to have their hair cut every two weeks in order to keep their "racing stripes" razor sharp. Likewise, many girls failed P.E. because they refused to dress for class. You see, changing into T-shirts or running might have messed-up their hair. The craziest thing was that their parents allowed them to continue failing, year after year!

Some parents spent more than two hundred dollars just for a pair of high-tech "pump-up" basketball shoes—often for kids who got winded just jogging to the cafeteria. I was afraid to ask how much they'd invested in the sport team jackets many students wore, even on the hottest of days.

As I watched the poor kids sweating in agony—but smiling smugly in the knowledge that they were in style—I realized that my parents had accomplished a lot more than simply saving money with all their "No's." They'd communicated to me—subtly but emphatically—that impressing people with what I wore would not be a priority for me. Preparing myself for university would be. They later lavishly spent every dime they had saved on my college education.

My mom and dad freed me from the tyranny of style. They taught me to have the courage to be myself, and to struggle to make of myself somebody great. By denying me so much, they gave me what mattered most.

The jet airplane took a little over five hours to fly from Oakland to Cleveland, carrying me on my yearly pilgrimage home for Christmas. In the ethereal world at 33,000 feet, the tranquil limbo between my harried life in California and the more sedate lives of my family in Ohio, I couldn't help but finally pause and reflect. An unrepentant vagabond, I marveled to find myself living where I lived, doing what I did.

It occurred to me that my parents, who were waiting to greet me at the airport, must be similarly amused to see who I'd become. And for the first time I realized that it was they who long ago had given me the freedom to choose my own path.

I remembered one incident which had seemed insignificant at the time, but which I finally recognized as a striking example of my parents' courageous restraint.

My mom and dad had visited me during my freshman year in college because I'd landed a big part in a Shakespearian play. (I played Dromio of Ephesus in *A Comedy of Errors*.) After the performance, I brought them backstage to meet the director. "Dave's made quite a splash in the theater department here," she commented effusively. "We can see he's going to make a wonderful addition to the Drama Department!"

My parents politely smiled, but I could tell they were stunned. They had assumed my acting was merely a hobby, that I'd major in something practical like business or engineering. In fact, my dad had once commented that any liberal arts degree was a total waste of time and money.

The following morning my parents took me out to breakfast before their long drive home. The conversation was uncomfortable, strained. I could tell they wanted to dissuade me from a career in the theater. They brought up the subject only once, though. "Well," my father said, carefully stirring his coffee, "I suppose you'll get a lot of big parts here, since the theater department is so small and unknown."

Mild encouragement, a bit of caution, but nothing more. How difficult it must have been for my parents to bite their tongues!

I soon gave up the theater on my own—thank goodness. (I wonder if I would have done so had my parents demanded it.) But there were many other times in my life when my mom and dad forced themselves to remain mute while I went ahead and made apparently outrageous decisions.

After graduation, for instance, I spent two years gallivanting through Spain. Upon my return, I accepted my first teaching job—in Texas of all places!—for a paltry $8,000 a year. Was I crazy?

In retrospect, I regret none of my choices. My many adventures, good and bad, prepared me well.

I consider myself fortunate indeed when I see some of my friends languishing in careers their parents chose for them; and when I witness students struggling at a sport or an instrument they hate, but their parents enjoy vicariously. My mom and dad insisted only that I guard my integrity and get a good education. The rest they left up to me. They let me follow my heart.

And that is why every Christmas, for as long as my parents live, my heart will always lead me back home, to them.

RAINBOW LINING

A t first it was my nightmare, then my curse, briefly my cross to bear, and finally one of life's greatest blessings.

I never chose to be gay. Indeed, I spent nearly two decades attempting to deny it, run away from it, pray it away…anything.

As a teen, I furtively scanned the ladies' bra and underwear sections of the Sears catalog, desperately trying to find the featured women sexy. What was the matter with me?

Later in the full throes of puberty, my gut would clench tightly whenever I saw an attractive boy. "No! No! No!" I pleaded, suppressing all my crushes.

In college, I once dared to confess my "dirty" thoughts to the dorm rector. The warm-hearted priest—who I now realize was gay, himself—tried to console me with the idea that longings were not evil in themselves; the implication being, unfortunately, that acting on them would be. I buried myself deep in the closet.

Deeper still because of AIDS. If I ever tried anything sexual with a man, I could never, ever give blood again, since the blood of all homosexuals was—and is—considered to be tainted. There could be no going back even if I just "tested the water" once.

Very deep, indeed, since I eventually became a teacher. Everyone knew that "gay" was synonymous with "pedophile." How could God make me a gifted educator and also make me gay? One evening my senior year in college, I walked around Notre Dame's Saint Mary's Lake, pleading with and berating God, sobbing.

I spent the next decade immersing myself in noble workaholism—becoming a columnist, a mentor teacher, a teacher trainer, a community activist, a hike leader, the member of multiple boards—all a pathetic attempt to run away from intimacy with myself or anyone else, and to convince myself and the world that, despite my terrible, secret shame, I was still a worthwhile human being.

When I turned thirty, however, I just grew tired of lying. I called Kaiser—from a phone booth, of course—and asked to meet with a counselor. "And I don't want you to put me with a gay therapist," I insisted.

Years later, I wrote that straight counselor a letter of thanks. He oh-so-gently nudged me out of the closet into the light of my life. "I can't tell you what you are, David" (knowing I'd have to be the one to tell myself), "but I can tell you it's time to stop running away. You need to get out and meet some gay people. They won't bite, you know."

And so I went on my first hike with the local gay and lesbian section of the Sierra Club. I was confused when I arrived at the trailhead. Although there was a fairly large group gathered, none of the hikers looked gay. (I guess I was expecting pink spandex with feathers.)

That first hike I turned my collar up, pulled my cap down, and just listened. One hiker complained about her rent, another about his boss. Three debated California politics. Two men who'd been together for 17 years bickered about whose turn it was to do the laundry. Why, these homosexuals were just ordinary people. They seemed happy! Who'd have thunk?

Many hikes later, I came to respect them—and, through them, myself. I learned to be able to say, "I'm gay," and still believe I was OK. When I confided to some of the older members that I still longed for a "normal" life, marriage with a woman, several replied, "That's what I did. And I became an alcoholic. Worse, I'll never forgive myself for what I did to my wife when I finally owned up to who I was."

I owe that group—my first of many gay and lesbian social groups—a great debt. I continue to lead hikes for them today.

Several hurdles remained. In a subsequent meeting with the therapist, I finally, haltingly, confided my most heinous secret: I found some of the young men in my classes attractive. I was terrified he'd have to inform the authorities and end my career.

That therapist did a marvelous thing. He looked at my angst-ridden face for a brief moment, and then burst out laughing. No, he guffawed. He took off his glasses, wiped his eyes, all the while saying, "Oh, David! Oh, David!" Finally, "I can see how this has tormented you! Well, let me be the first to let you know: teenagers are gorgeous! Do you think the straight teachers don't notice? You're allowed to notice too! I know you're a fine teacher, David. And you'll be even better if you just learn to accept yourself and relax."

Slowly, I did. Three years later, after working my painstaking way up the ladder of family and friends, coming out to the easiest ones first, there remained only my parents.

Mom initially just cried. "I've always pitied gay people," she said.

Dad, who was feeble and not always lucid at the time (I almost didn't come out to him), did another marvelous thing: He looked over at my pained face and Mom's tears, pulled himself off the couch, came to me placing my head in his hands, and said, "That must have been really hard. I'm proud of you!" Then, he kissed me on my forehead. I later recounted that moment in homage at his funeral.

Mom was a quick study herself. She attended the next local PFLAG (Parents, Families and Friends of Lesbians and Gays) meeting ("I cried the whole time, but they said I was doing very well") and to everyone's amazement, especially her own, she soon became an activist. (I eventually helped start a new local PFLAG chapter in my community.)

I returned home one day to a message on my phone machine: "David, I just got back from a bridge game. One of the other players made a horrible comment about a masculine woman in the room with cropped hair, and I just lost it. 'My son is gay,' I yelled at him. 'And I will not allow you to say such a homophobic remark in my presence.' You could have heard a pin drop! And I felt great! I can't wait for the next slur I hear."

But my favorite line of Mom's remains, "I pray every day that God will send you a boyfriend, David. It felt really odd at first, but I'm getting used to it."

I lead a charmed existence. And, part of that charm is being gay. No, I didn't choose to be gay. I finally chose only to live an authentic life, to be myself. (Which was, by the way, far better than putting on a damned cowboy vest!) Even all the tortured years in the closet, despite the deep scars they left, had their rainbow lining. Coming out forced me to plumb myself to my core, find a courage I doubt I would have otherwise, made me a better person and teacher, and introduced me to some of the finest people in my life—including and especially my partner, Edgar.

It's been a difficult journey, but in the end a grand adventure. I wouldn't have missed it for anything.

NEVER RIDE ALONE

Five hundred and eighty-five miles on a bicycle provided ample opportunity for reflection.

Along with 1,615 others, I participated in AIDS/LifeCycle 4, pedaling in seven grueling, emotional but ultimately inspiring days from San Francisco to Los Angeles. Together we raised nearly $7 million to fight the AIDS pandemic.

Along the way, a colleague's stinging criticism still rang in my ears. The rebuke had occurred during a retention meeting, when school administrators, counselors and I had discussed which of my students, because of their poor performance on grades, writing samples and standardized tests, ought to repeat the year. (Research still doesn't support that practice.) Just before I'd left, I'd tossed off a flippant complaint: "You know, if any of these kids had one decent parent who would follow through on anything, we wouldn't be having this discussion."

"That's terribly unprofessional," the principal responded in anger. "You don't know the situations of these parents. How dare you make such a sweeping accusation?" And, of course, he'd placed a subtle but definite emphasis on "you" because I had no children of my own.

Weeks later, as I rode my way south through the Salinas Valley and later along the California coast, the scolding echoed like some unwelcome tune I couldn't get out of my head.

I finally gave in and, rather than fight the memory, I examined it, pondering as best I could the nature of parenting. And, because I was on a bike, it seemed only natural to make what soon revealed itself to be a tortured comparison: Parenting is like riding AIDS/LifeCycle. The inadequacy of the simile itself, however, was my lesson.

Yes, it's true that the ride, like parenting, involved challenges, such as flat tires and hundred-mile days; as well as joys, such as a surmounted hill or a blessed tailwind. Then, the comparison fell apart.

The ride organizers assured everyone that "No one rides alone." From the moment I'd registered, I'd been guided by a "riding buddy," Susan, who had stayed in regular e-mail contact with me, watching over my fund-raising and training, dispensing advice, answering questions. She made sure I was ready for the challenge.

During the event itself, 405 volunteers supported the riders: roadies, cooks, doctors, bicycle mechanics. In fact, I couldn't ever stop, not even to savor a beautiful view, without a sweep vehicle pulling over within a minute or two to make sure I was OK. (It got annoying.) Along the route, outriders on motorcycles stationed themselves at every difficult or dangerous intersection, directing me with red flags and an encouraging word. Atop every steep hill and at the end of every long day, there was a crowd at the side of the road cheering, whistling, ringing cowbells.

Most endearing of all was the way everyone treated the last rider of the day. As he or she passed, the motorcycles fell in behind, providing a roaring escort. Ahead in camp, once "The last rider is approaching!" had been announced, everyone left their tents or tables to greet that exhausted rider with the most raucous welcome of all. None of us relaxed until all of us were safely home.

Well, raising children isn't like that. When wealthy suburban parents have their children ensconced safe in college, they don't drop everything to cheer on their struggling inner-city peers. When, at 2 am, a bleary-eyed mom tries to rock her sick infant to sleep, there's no sweep vehicle pulling over with the message, "You look like you could use some assistance." When a dad deliberates, "Do I force Tina to clean her room, or allow her to have one refuge truly her own?" there's no outrider pointing the way. When, after holding firm and saying "no" to too much social media or an unsupervised party, and then enduring their teen's ugly tantrum, there's no crowd cheering parents on, "Way to go!"

True, parenting, like the AIDS Ride, is a long, sometimes overwhelming challenge. The difference is that too many parents in our sick culture raise their children alone. And if, after more than a decade of struggle, some finally give up, I have to remember that, without all the support I received on the ride, I probably would have given up, too. I couldn't have made it to LA alone.

The next time I want to criticize a parent, I'm going to think about that.

THE FENCE

I pounded the nails with an unnecessary vengeance, since both the planks and the fence I was hammering them back on to—for the umpteenth time!—were riddled with rot and termites. I hated to look out my living room window at the fence grinning back with so many missing teeth. It made the complex shabby. Would the condo association management and board never manage to reach a consensus, levy the special assessment, and replace that damned fence?

So, I'd stormed out my front door once more, my pursed mouth bristling with nails. They slid through the soft wood with an unsatisfying ease, my blows only venting frustration at the Sisyphean task. I knew some nameless, malevolent teen would knock the planks off again soon enough, perhaps only to annoy his nameless long-suffering neighbor—me. Maybe he was even watching me right now with perverse pleasure. What was the matter with people? Why were some so incompetent, others so mean? That fence had become a symbol for all that was wrong with the human race. And so I battered it with yet another futile nail.

Finally, one Saturday afternoon when I was walking home, I turned the corner onto to my complex, and there he was.

A boy of about twelve was blithely kicking a soccer ball around the greenbelt between my house and the fence. To my horror, when the miscreant had placed the ball just right, he launched it hard against the fence, which shuddered at the impact; but, at least this time, didn't lose a plank. Then the boy deftly retrieved the ball, and began the set up for his next kick.

"Why that little…," I muttered, my eyes narrowing, my fists clenching, my breath now heaving. I was going to give that kid a tongue-lashing the likes of which he would not soon forget!

Then, I stopped cold, detained by a flashback to my own childhood: Old Mister Johnson had come screaming out his front door any time my friends and I had even inadvertently stepped upon his manicured lawn. Honestly, I suspected the geezer spent his whole retirement peering out his living room window, just waiting to pounce. At the time, he'd made me so mad! Now, in retrospect, he seemed only pathetic.

Had I become pathetic, too? I watched the boy for a moment as he practiced intently. I looked around the neighborhood, realizing the only other place he had to play was the street. And I thought of all the columns I'd written bemoaning kids' lethargy and obesity. Here this boy was, doing exactly what he ought to be doing, and I'd been about to shriek at him.

Instead, I continued walking slowly up the path to my front door, marveling at the boy's ability. As I passed him, he paused briefly. I waved, and he waved back.

"Having fun?" I asked.

"Yeah." Then he kicked the ball at the fence.

And I laughed.

Late Sunday morning I again stepped out my front door laden with hammer and nails—humming. Strangely enough, that bedraggled fence now represented all that was at once both maddeningly imperfect and oh-so-right with the world.

I was disappointed when a new one finally replaced it.

THE GENERAL

"I have these discounted tickets to paintball, Dave," my young neighbor, Danny, implored, "but my mom says I can go only if you take me."

I was flattered by the trust Danny's mom placed in me, but found myself in a quandary. I disagreed with making a game out of something as horrific as war and killing, much less initiating a youngster into it.

Danny pleaded with his puppy-dog eyes, though, and I caved. Implacable I'm not.

Once there, Danny and I donned some blue coveralls and helmets, grasped our pump-action paint-ball guns, and followed our team out into a huge, dim warehouse.

There we beheld an eerily realistic inner-city battleground, littered with fake bombed-out buildings and streets. The red team congregated menacingly on the opposite side. I figured I'd just dodge here and there, shoot off a few random paintballs at nothing, and pretend to have a good time while trying to protect Danny from the worst.

Within ten seconds of the start of the first game, "Ouch!" No one had told me paint balls hurt. The next two short games were no different, both Danny and I quickly "dying" without firing a single shot. This was no fun.

A teammate finally explained: "There are two guys on the red team behind that far pillbox with their own custom, telescopically-sited, high-powered paintball rifles. We don't stand a chance!"

"Why those little…," I replied. "That's not fair! OK you guys," I called out to the rest of the blues, "let's have a strategy this time and take those jerks out!"

I instructed the main body of our team to advance up the center making as much commotion as possible. I then sent two lithe teens creeping their way up the right, while Danny and I slithered up the left. I figured, once in place, the other two could set up a crossfire, allowing Danny and me to storm the pillbox from behind.

When I signaled the teens to commence firing, however, they chickened out, merely cowering beneath a crumbling low wall. Thus, when Danny and I broke cover, the snipers easily cut us down.

The next game I became frustrated, reckless. An assault team of one (just call me "Rambo"), I snuck up on the snipers, then charged, shrieking. I dove over the pillbox, rolled into an upright position, and pumped off two quick shots, eliminating my targets.

The moment of triumph was short-lived. I was now behind enemy lines and completely exposed. The rest of the red team opened up, riddling me with paint balls.

When it was all over, the umpire, who'd been observing all the games from above, slid down his ladder and ran over to me. "Hey General," he called out. "Listen, that was really good! I'm forming my own competitive paint ball team, and I'm wondering if you'd be interested in joining."

Covered in paint, I pulled off my helmet and replied, still panting heavily, "No, I'm afraid not. I'm philosophically opposed to this whole thing."

Danny didn't believe me, either.

ASHER

He was just a damn, dumb cat.

I'd sworn I'd never adopt another one. After all, the food the United States lavishes on our pets (many of them obese!) could feed the world's starving many times over. The health care we provide them remains out of reach even for millions of Americans. No, no pets for me!

Then a stray tabby kitten plopped itself onto my lap, purred, and convinced me to abandon yet another of my "nevers." I named him Asher since he was gray, and I'd been reading Chaim Potok's *The Gift of Asher Lev*.

Ours was a strained relationship. Asher nearly opened my jugular during the first—and last—flea bath I gave him. And, although I'd neutered him forthwith (thus collecting a dear price for my irrational hospitality), he sparred with every other cat in the neighborhood—and too often lost. His most shameful scar forever marked a nasty abscess on his butt. (I'd told him to return with his shield, or on it!)

Worst of all, Asher sprayed urine throughout my house. It began with the first of his many bladder infections. However, once he realized how furious the spraying made me, it became his favorite expression of anger, anxiety, or depression. His favorite target was the back door and the stove. (You haven't lived until you've enjoyed the lovely aroma of baked cat urine.)

I don't want to know how much I wasted on that damn, dumb cat's vet bills. I once threatened the vet through gritted teeth, "Listen, you need to cure these infections once and for all, or I'm going to have him destroyed!" The others in the waiting room clutched their pets to their breasts with wide-eyed outrage.

Still, there were so many sweet moments. Asher writhed on the ground with purring ecstasy every evening upon my return home. He basked under my desk lamp while I composed columns, waiting patiently for my absent-minded caresses between paragraphs. Afterward, he joined me outside beneath a tree, teaching me to appreciate the evening, the moment, his tail tapping languidly with Buddhist contentment.

Now I sit there alone. Asher disappeared for a week, finally crawling his way back home emaciated, dehydrated, with some sort of internal malady. Despite two visits to the vet, he died four days later, next to my desk.

Queen Elizabeth II wrote, "Grief is the price we pay for love."

Oh, Asher was just a damn, dumb cat; but as I placed him in the grave I'd dug in the shade of an old oak, I realized how good he'd been for me during our fourteen years together. He had not only provided me so much to complain about, but he'd forced me, still a bachelor and despite my stubborn logic, to be responsible to and for another. "It is the time you have wasted on your rose," the fox explained in Antoine de Saint Exupery's *The Little Prince*, "that has made your rose so important."

I miss Asher.

I wonder how many of our children, growing up in our callous, selfish culture, might learn lots of important lessons about life, love and responsibility by similarly caring for a stray cat or dog.

Never fear: Most don't urinate everywhere.

HUBRIS

I'd been a Sierra Club hike leader for over fifteen years. Yup. I knew most of the Bay Area trails like the back of my hand, and many others in the Sierras almost as well.

So, when along one of those trails a hiker I was leading asked if I'd ever been lost, I chuckled condescendingly to everyone in the group, then related Daniel Boone's famous answer: "No, I've never been lost, but I have been darned bewildered for several days!"

After the polite laughter subsided, I expounded on the different gradations of lost. "For example, there's the whoops-I-passed-the-turn-off-but-this-way-is-longer-yet-more-beautiful kind of lost; the I'm-not-sure-exactly-where-I-am-but-know-this-path-will-eventually-get-me-home kind of lost; and the I-can't-find-the-trail-but-there's-only-one-way-out-of-this-canyon kind of lost. You see, when you've been hiking for a long as I have, you inevitably find yourself somewhat lost every now and again. That's part of the fun!"

Wouldn't you know it, later that afternoon all of us were gathered around the map, exhausted, everyone pointing to a different spot as we desperately tried to figure out just where we were on the map (or, if we were even still on it). And then the same jerk who'd asked the question earlier looked over at me and smirked, "So, Dave, what kind of lost is this?" A moment later, twisting the knife, "Are we having fun yet?"

Whenever I get too full of myself, the gods usually conspire to bring me down like that.

Another time, when I was working on my scuba certification, I had to practice "finning" in a pool with my fellow divers. With our hands on a partner's shoulders, we used the large fins strapped to our feet to kick as hard as we could and attempt to push each other to the opposite side of the pool in a friendly, fun competition.

Unfortunately, I was paired with an older, rather, um, portly woman. It really wasn't fair, especially if you considered what great shape I was in at the time. (When you'd been running for as long as I had….) So as not to embarrass the poor thing, I decided to go easy on her.

That woman quickly slammed me back into my side of the pool. "Oops! Sorry!" she said oh so politely.

I demanded a rematch, claiming feebly that I'd not been ready. But she won again. And again. Finally, she let me win. There's nothing worse than pity!

Oh, yes, the gods must have had a hearty laugh at my expense that time. Not that I didn't deserve it.

The worst incident, however, was the softball game. I'd invited two out-of-town guests to come watch me play, and—if I do say so myself— I was playing mighty fine that evening. Indeed, in two innings three balls had soared out to me in center-right, and I'd fielded them all handily, including one amazing diving catch. "Nothing gets by old Ellison," I muttered as I nonchalantly threw the ball back in. "Yup. When you've been playing ball for as many years as I have…."

I saw the next ball leave the bat, once again headed straight towards me. "Another out," I gloated as I sauntered into position.

The ball hit me in the forehead. Wouldn't you know it, there I was, blinded by stars, flailing around on my knees, one hand holding my head, the other groping frantically everywhere for the damn ball.

My friends were quite impressed.

Yes, of all the sins the Greek gods of old forbade, excessive pride was the worst. They called it "hubris," and took a special, malevolent pleasure in punishing it.

I know such things because, well, when you've been studying history for as long as I have….

A NOBLE TRAGEDY

I've climbed Mount Everest. Struggling desperately for breath and consciousness, I gazed below at a gathering storm that would nearly kill me, and would claim some of my friends. I'd spend the rest of my life wondering if my presence on that mountain had caused their deaths.

I've crossed the Hellespont with Alexander, the Alps with Hannibal, the Rubicon with Caesar, the Pacific with Magellan, even the Rockies with Sacagawea—both triumph and disaster awaiting most of them on the other side.

I've witnessed the battles of Cannae, Gettysburg and Stalingrad. I've watched transfixed while Atticus Finch futilely defended Tom Robinson, Othello tragically strangled Desdemona, Theodora boldly saved Byzantium, and Sophie made her terrible choice.

Deep in the heart of windswept Mongolia, Genghis Khan showed me his sacred mountain, source of his strength. Afterward, I rode with him as he ruthlessly created the largest empire the world has ever seen, then made of it a Camelot of open trade, religious freedom, the world's first meritocracy where a man was judged not by his name or birth, but his character and skills. However, like all empires then and now, I watched it falter, then crumble into dust, leaving only an enduring legacy of ideas.

Ah, but it's those ideas and the questions that gave them birth that are immortal!

I've long pondered how to reconcile the apparently conflicting notions of equality and liberty, individualism and community, dogma and existentialism, republicanism and federalism, reason and faith, idealism and pragmatism.... Perhaps wisdom comes with the recognition that, in this imperfect world, we can never find a happy balance between any of them. No, we must make do with tortured compromises, best guesses, callow mistakes, a panorama not of black and white but messy grays, and ultimately the realization that life is too often a tragedy.

Literature tells the story of this noble tragedy. And it's by reading it that I, in one still-incomplete lifetime, have seen and done so much, met all those fascinating people, and confronted so many of life's issues, most of them far beyond my own narrow experience.

Reading enables me to touch immortality: to see the world through so many other people's eyes, both living and long-dead, watch them face excruciating moral dilemmas; and, if I haven't yet learned from their mistakes, perhaps I can at least one day accept my own failures more graciously.

Thomas Jefferson warned of reading's importance in a country like ours: "Democracy depends upon a nation that reads."

Malcolm X reminisced how literature transformed his life as well, in prison. Curled up on the floor next to the bars of his cell, reading late into the night by the garish light down the passage, "I never felt so free in my life."

Reading makes one both interested and interesting. It's one of life's greatest pleasures, one of a citizen's most important responsibilities.

Which is why I learned recently with such horror of America's declining culture: One in four adults didn't read a single book last year. And the national average dropped in the last seven years from ten books per year to just four.

Meanwhile, too many teachers chasing ever more elusive test scores feed their students worksheet after worksheet, instead of story after story, novel after novel. They're creating, at our bidding, a generation of Americans who'll hate reading.

Some day, many centuries hence, someone somewhere will read of this, and shake her head at the tragedy—but it won't be a noble one.

FAILURE

Early one summer morning, I sat waiting for my drawing class to begin, giddy as a kindergartener the first day of school. I had my freshly-sharpened pencils and charcoal sticks arrayed before me, as well as a giant drawing pad propped up on an easel, its blank page seeming to beckon my first creation.

This class would fulfill a life-long dream. Although I'd never displayed any artistic talent, I'd always wanted to draw. I'd imagined how wonderful it would be to stop along a hiking trail and, with meditative perception, recreate the panorama of trees and hills. Or, while traveling on a train, to surreptitiously sketch the face of a fellow passenger, capturing with just a few, deft strokes the depth of his elusive personality.

As I waited for the class to begin, I jotted down notes for this story, anticipating its major points: how it's never too late to learn; how important it is to not be afraid to make mistakes because they're what teach us; how, with dogged effort, anyone can succeed, even at drawing.

After a lengthy course overview, the professor finally assigned the first task: develop hand-eye coordination by making a "blind" outline drawing of my hand—that is, without taking my eyes off my hand to check the drawing until I was done. What fun!

I finished five minutes later, looked over at my first work, and burst out laughing.

The next day I moved on to drawing a shoe, a cow skull, even deer antlers, my portfolio of unrecognizable squiggles growing, my laughter becoming more forced, finally disappearing all together.

By the end of the week my classmates and I had graduated to sketches of a skeleton, celebrating afterward with our first "art walk," a stroll around the class to admire each other's work. Everyone else's sketch had captured, if not the precise form of that stupid skeleton, at least its artistic essence. Mine alone stood out as little more than the pathetic attempt of a no-longer-giddy kindergartener. It was, if I do say so myself, awful.

Next, the professor sat the skeleton in a chair, adding a third dimension to our challenge. I groaned, but did my best. Nonetheless, each attempt got worse until my every stroke became physically painful, my stomach clenching ever tighter. It was agony.

I gave up on the skeleton and focused instead on the chair. Certainly I could at least draw a chair!

No, I couldn't. I slunk home, never to return.

So, that class and this story didn't turn out as planned. I didn't learn to draw. But, I did experience something important: humiliating failure.

It's the same failure some of my students suffer as they struggle to write a cogent essay or to solve a math problem. I realize now as never before that, unless they occasionally recognize improvement and accomplishment, learning for them will similarly become, not just torturous, but impossible. The difference is, they can't run away.

Since then, I've tried to remember to help all my students to know at least some small measure of success.

And that has become my art.

MOUNTAINS, MOTHERS, AND MURDER

I dropped my backpack with a groan next to a small alpine lake at 10,400 feet, somewhere in Kings Canyon National Park. John, aged 63, was leading Tina and me on what would turn out to be a glorious death march. We'd been hiking cross-country since dawn, a day's grueling trek from the nearest trail, and had already crossed two high passes. White Pass still loomed somewhere 1,200 vertical feet above, and I was exhausted.

I suddenly recalled a phone call I'd made to my mother so many years before when, as a freshman in college, I'd felt similarly overwhelmed.

"Well, Dave," she'd responded unsympathetically, "these are the moments that separate the men from the boys."

Chastened, I shouldered my pack and rejoined John and Tina who were correlating a topographical map with the off-trail backpacker's bible, Steve Roper's *The Sierra High Route*.

"We need to pass these three tarns (small, alpine ponds) first," John proffered pointing to the map, "and then proceed from there to the pass. I think they're just beyond that steep ridge," and he set off.

Since John had been exploring the Sierras before either Tina or I had been born, we followed faithfully, albeit reluctantly.

An hour and a half later we made the pass, then traversed a quarter mile of talus (loose boulders) to Red Pass, from where we enjoyed a breathtaking panorama.

"Look to the right of the pyramid-shaped peak beyond that far valley," John instructed, spoiling Tina's and my brief moment of triumph. "Tomorrow, if I can find it, we'll cross Frozen Lake Pass there, at 12, 300 feet. We'll have to climb up a thousand feet of talus to reach it. Roper wrote it's the most challenging pass in the Sierras...."

I turned to Tina and mumbled, "As soon as John gets us back to a trail, let's kill him!"

Nonetheless, just after noon the following day, the three of us reached the elusive pass. My lungs were heaving, my feet were throbbing, my shins bleeding. Yet, I turned to John and gasped, "Thank you, John."

Afterward, Tina, John and I gratefully followed the John Muir Trail back to civilization.

As I thought of the new school year beckoning like another daunting pass before me, it occurred to me that education is a lot like backpacking. At least, the analogy enables me to offer students some apt advice as they struggle their way through what must often appear like the wilderness of school:

First, find a hard teacher like John, someone older and more experienced who's studied the texts, and who will dare to lead you beyond where you believed you could go, farther even than you thought you wanted to go.

Next, throw away any silly notions that all learning ought to be fun. No, like backpacking, acquiring knowledge and skill requires determined effort—step by dogged step, essay by painstaking essay, test by interminable test.

Don't go it alone, though. If you study with your classmates, they'll motivate you when the going gets tough, protect you from silly, perhaps even dangerous errors, and help the miles fly by. Before you know it, you'll look up and find yourselves at a summit—an aced exam, a completed project, graduation. And, oh what a glorious view from the top!

Turns out, hard-working students and intrepid backpackers share two apparently contradictory emotions: a keen sense of self-satisfaction, and a profound humility before the wonder and beauty of Creation. The journey is difficult, but worth it.

So, welcome back to school. Take a big breath, shoulder those backpacks...and listen to your mothers.

John woke Tina and me up at 4:15 a.m. again. This would be the final day of our trek, so my groan was a little less enthusiastic than usual.

I crawled out from the tent shivering to discover the previous afternoon's rainstorm had led to a crisp, clear night. The Milky Way still glowed majestically above our campsite at Vidette Meadow.

A half hour later we were already underway, finding our cautious steps with the light of our headlamps. A mere 14 miles stood between us and real food, real beds, real toilets; and if we pushed, we could be out in time for a restaurant lunch.

We followed Bubb's Creek, rushing its way to join the South Fork of the Kings River. Mars, nearing its closest approach to Earth in history, glinted like a red beacon just above the crest. And, in spite of my professed angst for the trial of this trip to be over, I found myself tarrying.

Just below a rocky ledge that had appeared along the trail, we discovered a breathtaking waterfall. We dropped our packs in silence and shared a cold breakfast. The first rays of the sun touched the ridge high above us, and I became overcome with emotion.

Unbidden, some long lost poetry welled up in my breast: "Every valley shall be exalted, and every mountain made low. And the crooked made straight, and the rough places plain." (*Isaiah* 40: 4-5).

I'll always cherish that moment. Afterward, I prayed a silent thank-you to Mrs. Petruziello, my high school choir director, who'd forced me to sing those beautiful words. They became, as my college professor, Dr. Rogers, later explained, "So much grain stored against a winter we never expect to come."

With this in mind, a previous, seemingly inconsequential incident along the trail took on new significance.

Two days before, John, Tina and I had been caught in a sudden downpour, and had taken shelter beneath a stand of pines. To pass the sodden time, we took turns reciting our favorite poems. John shared one by A.E. Housman, Tina another by Mary Oliver, and I Chief Seattle's letter to President Pierce: "Great Chief in Washington sends word that he wishes to buy our land. How can you buy or sell the sky, the warm of the land? The idea is strange to us. We do not own the freshness of the air nor the sparkle of the water. Every part of this Earth is sacred to my people."

Our words transformed what might have been a pathetic, dreary moment into a heart-warming afternoon of thoughtful camaraderie. Such is the power of poetry: to express deeply felt emotions; and, when shared, to bind us all together with the comforting realization that we all experience similar fears, longings, and joys. I wondered what it would be like to find oneself in a moment of great feeling or trial, but to have no poetry to call upon. Life would be a lonely, soulless pilgrimage, indeed.

Right then, by the waterfall, the prophet's ancient words still echoing in my heart, I understood the awesome opportunity/responsibility we teachers have to impart our world's greatest poetry—both sacred and secular—to our students. Their winter will come, and we need to prepare them for it.

John interrupted my musings. "Shall we?" he said, pointing down the trail.

I nodded and hoisted my pack. I cast one last wistful glance at the waterfall and the ridge, and then hurried after John and Tina; for, to borrow from Robert Frost, "The woods are lovely, dark and deep." But I had "promises to keep, and miles to go before I sleep. And miles to go before I sleep."

LORI

S ome of my friends I chose. Most, however, have come into my life unanticipated, apparently by chance, perhaps by Providence. No matter, all are gifts.

Lori Bierwagen was such a gift. She first wrote me responding to one of my columns—probably lamenting the state of children and schools these days, or scolding me for another grammatical error. (Her native language was German.) I replied, and so, letter by letter, our friendship developed. When, due to advanced arthritis and a stroke, Lori moved to a small retirement facility, I started to visit her.

During many of our occasional chats, Lori often reminisced about her fascinating, long life. And when she finally died, it fell to me to write her obituary—yet another gift: the perfect exercise for me, now, almost sixty years old, in a better position to appreciate both her life and mine.

Lori was born in 1922, in Marburg-Lahn, Germany, a cobble-stone university town of 25,000, complete with its own castle on a hill overlooking a lazy river and lush forests beyond. She shared a large house and beautiful garden with her parents and five siblings. At ten years old, while caring for a new-born sister, Lori already knew her life's calling: to become a nurse for infants.

Her idyllic childhood came crashing down with Hitler's rise.

Her father hated fascism. "He just wanted everyone to be able to live how they wanted to, without anyone, especially the government, telling them what to do or not to do," Lori reminisced.

Her 17-year-old brother, however, perhaps as a naïve act of teenage rebellion, joined the SS, Hitler's dreaded secret police. Aghast, her father slapped him, and the boy fled screaming, "You'll never see me again, father!" True to his word, he died in World War II.

Meanwhile, another brother joined The White Rose, an anti-Nazi student organization. This led to his arrest, torture, and forced conscription. When Lori visited him in boot camp, he tried to reassure her. "Never fear! As soon as they send me to the front, I'll hold my trigger finger up over the trench and get it shot off. Then they'll have to send me home."

It didn't work. He died, too.

The war was hard in other ways on Lori and her family. Everything was rationed. "We were allowed one ounce of butter and one of meat per week. Like everyone else, we sold our valuables to farmers for food."

Then, on March 27th, 1945, at 7 a.m. (Lori had an incredible memory), the air-raid siren rang through the town, even though there were no planes in the sky. The Americans had arrived. "We were relieved in a way. We'd worried the Russians would get to us first. And, oh my, the Americans were so well groomed!"

Nonetheless, when she learned of the decree not to speak to any of them, Lori muttered, "Well, good! Who'd want to?"

The Americans commandeered her home, and forced her and her family into a tiny, two-room apartment where they subsisted on horse flesh. It was on an errand for horse fat that the butcher learned of Lori's training as a nurse, and offered her a job caring for his infant daughter. Reluctantly, Lori accepted, even though the child was under quarantine for Diphtheria.

And so began Lori's long career.

A few years later, Lori thought to apply for another job, this time with an American colonel. When she opened the door to the interview, however, she spied nearly fifty other women waiting, and so she closed the door and turned to leave.

Where are you going?" a man asked. (The colonel himself, as it turned out.)

"Oh, this colonel surely will find someone among such a large crowd. He doesn't need me."

The colonel insisted on taking down her information "just in case." Sure enough, none of the other women possessed Lori's charm or her special training with premature babies. (Ha! I'd been a preemie!)

The colonel's car came to pick her up a few days later. Lori took with her one uniform and one change of shoes to what would become her new family. She greeted everyone haltingly with some of the few English words she could remember from school, "I am very pleased to make your acquaintance."

Two-and-a-half-year-old Billy replied, "I don't yike you!" When Lori first beheld tiny Pam, however, "It was love at first sight!" Soon, even Billy had changed his tune to "I yuv you, Yori!"

When Lori took Billy, Pam, and newborn Debbie through town, neighbors called out, "There go Lori's kids!" The three children called her "mother" for the rest of her life.

Lori eventually had to move on, and, due to excellent references, her early career took her to families in France, Italy, England, and even The Bahamas.

But it was Billy, Pam, and Debbie she missed. Many years later, she'd finally saved enough to see them in El Paso, Texas. Little did she know that this brief visit would lead to jobs with other American families, a long-distance correspondence with a Californian whom she'd marry, several head-nurse positions in Bay Area hospitals, and eventually, one day after she'd retired and buried her husband, a letter to me.

Despite being bed-ridden during her final years, at 93 Lori maintained an active intellectual life, reading voraciously, savoring opera and old movies, participating avidly in a twice-a-week group phone discussion, and never missing an episode of *Jeopardy* or *Are You Smarter than a Fifth Grader?* (I quickly learned never to visit or call when those shows aired.)

Her sense of humor remained intact as well. After a nearly fatal bout of Pneumonia when she became impatient with her slow recovery, Lori remarked dryly, "You know, I'm not 75 any more!"

Nonetheless, Lori longed for death. "I'm ready to return to God," she admitted late one afternoon, sustained to the end by her devout Catholic faith.

I fell in love with Lori.

She taught me much: That Life, if we have the courage to heed its call, may lead us on to many adventures, far beyond our wildest imaginings. That Karma truly does exist because, if we shower those around us with love, especially children, they will repay us tenfold. That, even in the face of declining health, old age, increasing pain and discomfort, if you have faith in something greater than yourself, you can still possess an overriding gratitude and joy.

Good things to remember at any time, whether you're almost sixty or not.

THE HOMECOMING

"What would they think of us?"

After twenty-six years, my college roommate, Eric, finally dragged me, one of The University of Notre Dame's prodigal sons, back to our alma mater for a football weekend.

I'd often begged Eric, if I ever returned like so many visiting alumnae, sporting flowered Bermuda shorts and a pot belly, he should, please, just shoot me; and, Eric had requested the same.

In that one respect, we'd both come back in triumph, wearing only green sweatshirts and slim jeans. We reminisced over dinner in the South Dinning Hall, surrounded by students, so terribly young. "What do they think of us?" I wondered. Then, a moment later, "What if the students we once were could see us as we are now? What would they think of us?"

We brooded in silence.

Eric had spent the majority of his undergraduate years ensconced in the library, overwhelmed by the fierce competition of the pre-med program. "I learned to memorize," he recalled sadly, "and enjoyed very little of it."

Nonetheless, he'd since become the paragon of the Notre Dame alumnus: still a devout Catholic, the chief physician at his Midwest clinic, a devoted husband and father. And, of course, a loyal Fighting Irish fan.

Eric was also facing his second divorce, this time from a woman who, although she cared for him, was in love with a woman. What would the Eric of old think of him now?

I, on the other hand, had rarely finished the readings for my humanities seminars, and had completed the many essays only in a frantic flurry, late at night. I'd been too busy with the chapel choir, the theater, the student union. Even so, it was at Notre Dame that I'd learned to love history and ideas, and to contemplate a career teaching them.

Since then, however, I'd consciously turned my back on so much of Notre Dame: the oppressive Catholic hierarchy, dogma, sexism, homophobia and guilt; the relentless pursuit of recognition and success; the irrational worship of sports (the new "opiate of the masses"), especially football. My wanderlust had led me far away in distance and thought.

Now I was nursing my own heartbreak, having recently abandoned with bitter No-Child-Left-Behind-induced disillusionment my love affair with public schools, taking a two-year leave of absence.

And, at the age of 48, although finally out of the closet, I'd still not found a life partner, much less created a family. What would the Dave of old think of me now?

How to explain to the cocky, naïve twenty-one-year-olds we were that they wouldn't be masters of their fate? That their futures, impossible to envision, would be shaped more by Providence/fortune than their bold decisions? That their most important choices would involve a commitment to someone or something; that each would require unforeseen risk and sacrifice, each would bring undeserved joy and grief? That the next quarter century would leave them cradling a baffling mess of gratitude, regret, and humility?

No, they—we—couldn't have understood. They'd have to learn for themselves. And they would. We did.

After Boston College had added its name to the litany of teams defeating The Irish that year, I watched the Notre Dame players kneel in front of their fellow students, all of whom had stayed to the bitter end. The band behind the team struck up the Alma Mater, and all sang, swaying together. It was as if the students were embracing the heartsick players with, "Yeah, you may be the losingest team in Notre Dame history, but you're still ours, and we love you."

In that moment of disgrace, I rediscovered my school pride. Life will humble us all, even the great Notre Dame. And so we must love each other—and our universities—in spite of everyone's inevitable failings.

Thus, mine was a wistful homecoming. I finally understood what Notre Dame thought of me, and I of her: For better and for worse, Notre Dame had helped make me who I was. Then, after my long, estranged absence, she'd welcomed me home, embracing me as one of her own, warts and all.

And I hugged back.

PART TWO: RAMBLING ABOUT SCHOOLS

"I had a lover's quarrel with the world."

ROBERT FROST

DON'T BE AN ACTOR

When I was a senior in high school, I landed the lead in the spring musical. I'd already learned to love the theater since it had finally gotten me out of my shell, convinced me I wasn't worthless after all, and filled me with an exuberant joy I'd never known before. Now I'd even gotten the lead! Why not make a life in the theater?

I approached the director, Mr. Murphy, with an eager, breathless question: "Do you think I have what it takes to make it as an actor?"

The answer, patently obvious to everyone but me, was a resounding "No!" Murphy was a wise and compassionate man, however. Rather than destroy me with a harsh truth, he replied with a sage one.

"That's the wrong question, Dave. Could you do anything else and still be happy?"

"Of course," I replied.

"Then, don't be an actor. It's just too hard."

Meanwhile, the first glimmerings of my real vocation had already made their debut.

In my U.S. History class, for instance, everyone had to make some sort of oral report. This was before I'd discovered the theater, when for me there was no nightmare more frightening than speaking in public.

Nonetheless, as I stood trembling before the class in order to explain Civil War General McClellan's ill-fated march up the Peninsula towards Richmond, latent gifts emerged of their own accord, in particular my flair for the dramatic and my knack for telling a good story.

McClellan could have ended the war easily if only, once across the Potomac, he'd unleashed his army pell-mell towards a city that was scarcely defended. Ah, but although McClellan—hapless soul!—was a genius at building an army, he was afraid to use it. He proceeded oh-so-cautiously (which I acted out, taking ponderous steps, my eyes anxious as I checked off each imaginary division behind me), allowing the Confederates time to prepare.

McClellan hesitated yet more when scouts reported Confederate regiment after regiment marching across a clearing. The truth was, there was only one regiment that kept running back around through the trees, regrouping with different flags, and marching through the clearing again.

I pantomimed that ruse out as well, utilizing the teacher's desk as my forest prop. Caught up in the story, I couldn't help myself.

When I was done, the class stared open-mouthed. (Who are you, and what have you done with that squeaking, stuttering Dave?)

The teacher, Miss O'Donnell, asked me afterward if I'd ever considered becoming a teacher.

"Ha!" I replied derisively.

The scene repeated itself seven years later in one of the first English classes I taught in Spain—a job I'd pursued, I claimed, only to make a living while in the country. I have no idea why the school hired me because, during the interview, I'd stuttered even worse in Spanish. As I approached the classroom and a gracious colleague wished me luck, "*G-g-gracias*" was I could muster. I was terrified!

A few moments later, I stared at thirty-five high school kids who gazed curiously back. Then, another miracle occurred: I broke into a grin and introduced myself—with a fluid, flawless Spanish I hadn't known I was capable of. Once again, something in my soul knew I was home.

Many, many years later, after a two-year leave of absence from teaching, I resigned from a plum job as Media Relations Manager for the San Francisco AIDS Foundation. Had I lost my mind?

No, I'd just finally realized that, even though teaching was a frustrating, exhausting, and maligned profession (like acting, just too hard), I couldn't do anything else and still be happy.

INLINGUA LANGUAGE SCHOOL

Santander, Spain

It was the very first class I'd ever taught. I was supposed to teach English as a Second Language at Inlingua, a Berlitz-like after-hours language school.

Inexplicably, the director had assigned me to an unruly bunch of ten middle-schoolers. Three previous, veteran teachers had given up in succession, vowing never to face the hellions again. I was too inexperienced to know I should have refused as well.

The first few days were disasters. My only achievement had been to cajole the kids on at least a few occasions to actually sit in their desks all at the same time. Getting them quiet remained an elusive goal.

Pablo was the worst. In spite of his soft, green eyes and cute, angelic face, he was the ringleader whose outbursts were the most disruptive, the most apparently defiant. If I could scare him somehow, make him fear me, the others might fall into line. But how? I spoke only beginning Spanish, the students little English at all.

I turned to my Spanish roommates and asked them how to say, "Be careful, buster!" Then I practiced the phrase over and over, endeavoring to feign Spanish fluency, and so earn the kids' respect.

The next class I deployed my secret weapon amidst the worst of the chaos. I approached Pablo and, jabbing a finger menacingly in his astonished face, uttered icily, *"Ten cuidado, hombre!"*

Pablo's green eyes grew large, and the other students turned and stared, similarly stunned.

I seized upon the ensuing, blessed moment of silence to add, "Now sit down and shut up! I've had enough!" They didn't understand a word, but they complied. Success! For years afterward I savored that scene as the beginning of my teacher preparation.

Truly momentous moments too often pass unnoticed. The real one occurred later that same class while I was attempting to rid the students of their deplorable accent: "dis," "dat," and "zurteen" instead of "this," that," and "thirteen." "You have to place your tongue beneath your teeth, blow some air and make it vibrate," I instructed. "Like this," I added, making an exaggerated sound like that of an engine revving up.

That was all Pablo needed. In an instant he'd fled his seat again, roving around the room with his tongue slobbering, popping wheelies like some sort of crazed drag racer. The others immediately followed suit, and, thus, it seemed chaos reigned anew.

Just before my simmering rage exploded, however, I noticed that every single student was finally making the "TH" sound correctly; and, in an instance of inspired madness, I joined the line of raucous students parading around the room, my tongue out the farthest. Eventually, the kids collapsed back into their seats, laughing uproariously. When they'd caught their breath, they turned back expectantly towards me. What was the next game?

Now, so many years in retrospect, I realize I didn't teach Pablo to respect me that day. Oh no! He taught me the best way to instruct him and his friends: Instead of suppressing all their energy, silliness and noise, I needed to call it forth, channel it, then unleash it. And, as, day by day, I slowly learned to do so, those students and I came to love that class.

The Pablos of the world are still my favorite students.

✳ ✳ ✳

"Is that a green box?"
"No, it isn't."
"Is that a red box?"
"Yes, it is!"

And so went my first classes at Inlingua. I followed the school's method: Forbidden to speak any Spanish in class, I'd model some new English expression, then instruct the ten or so students in class to practice a chain of identical questions and answers. Once they mastered that short "conversation," I'd introduce another.

It was an easy, structured curriculum. Even so, I soon felt constrained by The Method, and so sometimes resorted to brief Spanish explanations. This peccadillo usually saved some class time or clarified a difficult point. Every now and again, though, I'd get myself into trouble.

Once during an advanced class with teenagers, we came upon the expression "the last straw." I didn't want to digress into a long story about camels, so I simply tossed off a quick, literal translation, more than a bit smug about my emerging Spanish fluency. To my horror, pandemonium broke loose, many of the kids pounding their desks with wide-eyed laughter. As I was soon to learn, the Spanish word for "straw" is also the colloquial expression for masturbation. Oops.

My late-evening adult class posed the worst behavior problems. Although intent on learning English, they were often tired after a long day at work, and couldn't help but take advantage of their friendship with me. (We met once a month for dinner in the fishing quarter, evenings when the tables turned and I became their Spanish student.) They loved to see just how exasperated they could make me in class, conspiring to purposefully mangle some phrase or pronunciation, bursting out laughing only just before they drove me to distraction. I still miss them.

I was Inlingua's token American, the rest of the teachers hailing from Britain. Our different pronunciations created havoc whenever we switched classes. For example, the hapless students couldn't understand my "box" at all until I remembered to pronounce it "bawx." Or to say "bird" without including the "r."

As time passed, I unconsciously adopted my British colleagues' expressions and accent. (They insisted I was the one with the accent.) In fact, when I finally returned to the United States, I was shocked at my family's atrocious "hick" manner of speaking; as they were with my apparently uppity one. (Y'all know my next teaching job in Texas quickly cured me of tha-at!)

In one beginning adult class at Inlingua I'll always remember with chagrin, a student interrupted the lesson to ask pointedly if I were American. When I nodded proudly, he slammed his book shut and stormed out of the room.

Thus began the painful collapse of my American naiveté. But those long-lost Inlingua classes were also the beginning of my grand adventure which continues today; when I first fell in love with travel, languages, diverse cultures, different points of view, and the wondrous, overwhelming, infuriating but always rewarding life of a teacher.

SAINT LEO'S GRADE SCHOOL

San Antonio, Texas

I made a point of dressing casually. Young, idealistic, I rebelled against the pervasive image-conscious culture that judged a person by such a frivolous criteria as clothes. I typically sported faded corduroys, a striped polo shirt with a frayed collar, and a pair of dilapidated Keds. I would earn respect with my competence, my skills and ability.

Nonetheless, when parents dropped their children off and spied the slovenly character to whom they were entrusting their children, they weren't exactly assured. "He did go to college, didn't he?" they murmured apprehensively. All the hapless principal could offer in defense was, "He seemed OK during the phone interview."

I wasn't an easy new teacher for any principal to direct.

When Halloween came, for example, and everyone wore an outlandish outfit to school, I showed up in my best suit and tie. "I'm masquerading as a teacher," I explained with a smirk. The principal shook his head and shuffled away muttering to himself. That was his usual response to my antics.

A few weeks later, I interrupted my students' lunchtime keep-away game. "All right! All right! Give me the ball," I scolded in feigned anger, as if I'd caught the kids tackling again. Once I had the ball in hand, though, my frown gave way to a mischievous grin. "I'm it," I laughed, and took off running.

Well, I was fast. I kept that class at bay for nearly five minutes before cunning little Conrad blindsided me, and brought me panting to the ground. Then the kids showed no mercy. At the end of lunch, I limped disheveled past the principal, one Keds missing, dried grass hanging from my hair and stuffed down my shirt, my students prancing triumphantly around me. He shook his head and shuffled away, muttering to himself.

In the spring, it was my class' turn to perform at the PTA meeting, and so lure parents into attending. There would be no boring songs or puppet shows for us! No, I convinced my students we needed to do something really unique.

Little Jennifer took the stage. Reverently opening a ponderous text, she began to read "The Desiderata": "Go placidly amid the noise and the haste. . ."

Then, little by little, according to my meticulous directions, all hell broke loose on stage. A baby dropped his lollipop and wailed. His mother shrieked at him to stop. Bank robbers entered, shooting their cap guns, pursued by policemen blowing their whistles. Dogs barked. Elvis sang. And all the while Jennifer read, oblivious: "And whether or not it is clear to you, no doubt the universe is unfolding as it should...."

Meanwhile, Conrad slowly assembled a huge bomb in the center of the stage. In the end, there was a gigantic crash, the lights went out, silence prevailed. A few moments later the lights came back on revealing Jennifer serenely finishing her reading, "It is still a beautiful world . . ." while the rest of my students lay helter-skelter on stage in various grotesque poses of death.

I thought it was brilliant. The parents in attendance, though, after a stunned moment of disbelief, merely applauded perfunctorily. Hurt, I asked the principal what he thought of the performance. "Dave," he sighed in exasperation, "it was very . . . you." Then he shook his head and shuffled away, muttering to himself.

That was a compliment, right?

* * *

Dear Imelda,

I owe you an answer, even after all these years; and even though you probably have forgotten you ever asked me the question. Perhaps you don't even remember me, your sixth grade teacher. But I haven't forgotten you or your question, or the year we spent together in that sweltering Texan classroom. How could I forget my first year of teaching?

My friends had told me that my first year would be hell, and they weren't mistaken. I slaved each evening over homework and quiz papers. I sacrificed my weekends to create beautifully intricate lesson plans, only to abandon them by Wednesday. Worse, I did not yet know how to manage a classroom or discipline teenagers. Indeed, my voice was usually hoarse at the end of each day—not from lecturing, but from yelling to no avail.

The worst time, as you may recall, Imelda, was just after lunch. The class would return from recess all sweaty and excited, in no mood to be quiet or cooperate with anyone. Row by row, I would dismiss you to the restrooms. I needed to supervise the classroom, the water fountains, and the restrooms, all simultaneously. I usually wasn't very successful. (If only I had a dime for every water fight that year!)

And all the while I kept thinking to myself, "This isn't what I had in mind when I chose to become a teacher." Oh how I hated that quarter hour just after lunch!

It was at just such a moment that you asked me your question, Imelda. You must have noticed my impatient, anguished frustration. (Even now I still can't hide my moods from my students.) I wonder how long you watched me before you asked, "Mr. Ellison, are you happy?"

It was such a simple, yet profound question, the kind only the youth in all your innocence can ask. It caught me by surprise. "Right now, I really don't know," I responded lamely. Then I tried to turn the tables: "How about you, Imelda? Are you happy?"

Without a moment's hesitation you matter-of-factly responded, "Yes, Mr. Ellison, I am." And that was the end of our conversation.

Thirty-six years have swept by, Imelda. You're a middle-aged woman now—an engineer? A mother? A teacher? I, too, have grown up. I've lost a lot of hair, but learned a great deal about teaching. For example, I never lose my temper anymore. (Well, almost never.) Over the years, I've taught several thousand students. Many of them I've already forgotten. But, as I said, Imelda, I haven't forgotten you, or your question. I've always felt uncomfortable about my inability to respond as quickly or sincerely as you. Now, at last, it is fitting that I finally do. I was going to qualify my answer with "All things considered..." or "Overall...." But your simple question deserves better than that.

Yes, Imelda, I am happy. And wherever you are, I hope you still are too.

SAINT GERARD HIGH SCHOOL

San Antonio, Texas

I had just begun a new job teaching Spanish. Unfortunately, it was only an elective at St. Gerard, and so was considered a fluffy, easy course. My predecessor, for example, had been anything but strict. She'd rarely assigned homework, but had almost always given her students at least a "B," whether they could speak any Spanish or not, the latter being predominately the case. It seemed as if she had made an unspoken pact with her students: She wouldn't force them to really learn anything as long as they behaved. Everyone had appeared content.

Then I arrived. I announced the first day that I would give homework every night, and not one, but two quizzes a week. Also, after a brief introduction, I'd ban English in class.

Several students immediately dropped my class. The rest fought me bitterly. In fact, the principal remarked dryly at the first staff meeting that I had earned a dubious distinction: After only one week, my name had already made it to the bathroom walls.

Then a strange thing happened: My students learned some Spanish. In fact, they began to jokingly call out phrases like "*Cállate*" (Shut up!) and "*Date prisa*" (Hurry up!) in the lunchroom and hallways. Soon they were tossing around complete sentences; and for some of them, Spanish became a secret language they flaunted among their monolingual friends.

The clincher came in the spring when I organized a student-exchange program with a high school in Monterey, Mexico. Somehow— sometimes haltingly, often with grammar that made me wince—my students managed to communicate. I was so proud of them, and they were proud of themselves.

Don't get me wrong. The following year my students still came to my class groaning.

One dramatic, very important thing had changed, though: There were twice as many kids in my classes. All of them realized I'd push them hard, give them regular homework and quizzes. Yet they also knew they would learn. And so they came, complaining the whole while, but they came.

Despite all their protests to the contrary, kids really do want teachers to be hard on them. They want to learn. And they understand at least intuitively that holding them to high standards is the greatest compliment we can pay them; and that to do anything else is to betray them insidiously.

✻ ✻ ✻

As with the biblical story of the ten lepers, very few of my students ever return to say "Thank you." Still, over the years, some have written, and I treasure their letters. Whenever my commitment or confidence falters, I re-read them to remind myself that I've made a difference with at least a few of my students.

Out of all the letters, Christine's is my favorite. Perhaps this is so because I never expected to receive one like it. When I used to teach high-school Spanish, I'd hoped one of my students would one day write with the news she had passed the Advanced Placement Exam, or had gone on to become an ambassador to a Latin American country. Christine, however, related quite a different tale:

> *"...I also wanted to tell you about what happened to me last summer. Me, my mom, and my brother went to Martinique for a week. While we were there I had use for my knowledge of Spanish.*
>
> *"I was waiting for dinner to start, and I went for a walk on the beach. It was a beautiful night. Up behind me comes a nice-looking guy, and says, 'Parlez vous Francais?'*
>
> *"I said, 'No, I'm an American. I speak English. Do you speak English?' He said no. Then he asked me if I spoke Spanish. I said a little.*
>
> *"I hadn't spoken Spanish since school got out, but everything you taught me came rushing back into my head. We talked for hours in Spanish on the beach, and one thing led to*

another and, well, you know.... I mean, we didn't `YOU KNOW,'
but, well, we made-out for several hours! It was one heck of a
romance.

"Anyway, it would never have happened if I hadn't known
Spanish as well as I did, which was all because of you."

Now I can die in peace.

Seriously, I love Christine's letter. Not only does it bring a smile to
my face when I'm down; but I put it to good use in my Spanish classes. I
had often sought to motivate my students by reminding them how
important Spanish was—how, for example, the ability to speak it would
open up so many career opportunities.

This impassioned speech of mine was almost invariably greeted with
yawns. Then, I tried reading my students part of Christine's letter...
Worked every time.

I've tried to forget about Greg, how I let him down, leaving him
utterly alone. But the gift he gave me, a clay statue of an Aztec king, still
haunts me, denouncing me from atop my bookshelf, even as I write this.

At the time, the statue seemed an appropriate Christmas gift for a
high school Spanish teacher. Now I realize that nothing then was at it
first appeared.

Nearly everyone considered Greg the most fortunate, enviable kid on
campus. He was, after all, captain of the varsity track team. He excelled
in all his classes too, especially mine.

Nonetheless, behind his easy success and his captivating smile, Greg
hid a dark secret: He was gay. He never told me, of course, at least not
with words. Yet, in many other not-so-subtle ways, he revealed his
desperate longing for acceptance, for companionship.

I recall the day Greg first sought me out. It was after I had
admonished a classmate for jokingly insulting another with the epithet,
"Faggot!" "Pardon me," I chastised, "but that is very offensive, even in
fun. It's just as bad as any racial slur—expressing prejudice against
people who are different. I won't tolerate it in my class."

At the end of the period, Greg lingered to tell me I was the first
teacher he'd met who'd ever defended homosexuals. After that, he
stopped by often during lunch to chat, his questions becoming ever more

personal. Was I married? Was I presently dating anyone? He seemed pleased when, distracted, munching on my sandwich, I shook my head.

At Christmas, he timidly presented me with the statue. "I really like your class...and you, Mr. Ellison." Then he grasped me in a clumsy hug.

I was flattered. But I still didn't get it. Perhaps I was too young, too naïve. Or, maybe I really didn't want to comprehend since I couldn't yet accept my own homosexuality.

One evening a few weeks later, Greg came running up to me at a home basketball game. He insisted eagerly that I sit by him in the bleachers. But when I introduced him to the pretty woman at my side, his face collapsed. He stared at me wide-eyed, shaking his head in disbelief and betrayal. Then, after muttering a choked "Pleased to meet you, Miss," he fled the gymnasium.

At that awkward moment, I finally understood.

I wish I had followed him, or reached out at some other time. I should have broached the taboo subject, assured Greg he was not evil or weird, and above all, that he was not alone. But I was afraid. What closeted teacher wouldn't be in a small, Catholic, homophobic high school in Texas?

I tried to laugh-off the incident, to convince myself that I had misinterpreted Greg's behavior. He made it easy for me. He retreated obediently back into his own murky closet, and never approached me again. Indeed, he even went on to become prom king! Surely he was not gay.

But Greg's gift, the Aztec King on my shelf, still whispers otherwise. And he reminds me bitterly that, in the end, I didn't deserve him.

✳ ✳ ✳

Sandy was a quiet, studious senior in my high school Spanish class. Midway through the second semester, however, she mysteriously began to fail. She ignored my homework, and in class appeared strangely distracted. Even her shy smile had fled, leaving her morose, unhappy.

"What's the matter, Sandy?" I asked several times. Silence. "You know, don't you, that an "F" will prevent you from graduating? There's still plenty of time to catch up. Come on, Sandy! Don't drop the ball so close to the finish!"

She just sighed heavily, shrugged, and looked away. I asked around, but, although her other teachers were similarly concerned, they were equally befuddled. Against their better judgment, I called Sandy's father. He merely heaped obscenities on both Sandy and me.

One day Sandy disappeared. "She's in the hospital," answered one of the nuns in a furtive whisper. Yet, neither the good sister nor anyone else would elaborate. The secrecy made me both worried and intrigued.

The truth—which Sandy later revealed to me herself— was worse than all my awful imaginings. Several months earlier she'd found herself pregnant. Overawed by the moralistic atmosphere of our Catholic school, where it was forbidden to discuss contraception, she'd been too afraid to confide in anyone. Even when she became seriously ill, she sought no help, preferring to guard her terrible sin in desperate, helpless silence.

Sandy finally collapsed at school one morning, and was rushed to the hospital, unconscious. The interns immediately recognized she was pregnant. They also discovered that her baby was dead. Inexplicably, its corpse had not been spontaneously aborted, but had remained in her womb, atrophying. The resulting blood poisoning had nearly killed her. Less than an hour after she entered the hospital, doctors performed an emergency hysterectomy. Sandy was seventeen years old.

When she awoke, she wished she were dead. Her father, repeatedly calling her a whore, expressed the same desire.

Nonetheless, Sandy telephoned me only a few days later. "Mr. Ellison, I want to graduate. Will you tutor me?"

I still recall Sandy's slow, arduous steps down that sterile corridor to the hospital sunroom, where we worked. I remember how she fought though the pain and the drugs to concentrate on conjugations, and to complete my assignments.

Most of all, I cherish the image of her later receiving her diploma. Her timid smile again adorned her face, and the entire school community rose to greet it with a standing ovation.

Although it seemed all had forsaken her, Sandy had persevered. She'd transformed shame into self-respect, tragedy into triumph, a "Scarlet Letter" into a "Red Badge of Courage." Now, whenever I attend a graduation, I remember Sandy, and the lessons she taught us all.

THE GOLDEN AGE

New Haven Unified School District
Union City, California

When Guy Emanuele finally retired, he'd become the longest-standing superintendent in California history: a twenty-two year legacy of visionary leadership. He'd also transformed one of the state's worst districts into one of the best.

Guy started teaching at-risk students English in Room B-14 at Barnard-White Middle School (the same room where I worked many years later. We were both Notre Dame grads, too!) After a few difficult years, he went camping with several close colleagues; and, one night over a campfire, they broached a depressing, but pressing topic: New Haven Unified was an abysmal school district. And it was the poor, disproportionately minority kids who fared the worst. "That ain't right," they agreed. Then, after an uncomfortable silence, "We should change that."

Guy led the way. Over two decades, he worked his way up through various positions of leadership—counselor, union president, assistant principal, principal, district office administrator—until finally he became superintendent. Then, he surrounded himself with other like-minded administrators (several from that long, lost campfire), a dream-team of determined competence, all committed to establishing high standards for all. Together, they rolled up their sleeves, and got to work.

It wasn't pretty, at least not at first. Their first job was to get rid of the chaff, and there was plenty of it. Their ruthless axes fell, mercilessly dismissing incompetent/lazy teachers and administrators. Similarly, they expelled any students who were more interested in disruptions, fights, or drugs than in getting an education. (Truth be told, a few babies were lost with the bathwater.)

Meanwhile, Guy pushed the school board to pursue a series of community bonds to refurbish all the schools and equip them with the latest technology, computers in every classroom.

And all the while, Guy emphasized teachers. He raised their salaries to among the highest in the county, aggressively recruited the best college graduates, then trained and supported them well—focusing on a select cadre of mentors to lead the district. He needed them to implement the revolutionary pedagogy he had in mind.

Guy knew that tracking—separating students into apparently homogeneous ability groups (the bluebirds, the redbirds and the crows)—was the standard, convenient practice, but heinous, nonetheless. The crows, supposedly the kids with the least ability, were too often just disadvantaged and so behind, but no less intelligent than anyone else. The trouble was, once identified as a crow, usually in the earliest grades, these kids rarely escaped to the upper groups. The teachers didn't believe in them, and they didn't believe in themselves.

Emerging research indicated that heterogeneous grouping (keeping everyone together), although more challenging, worked out better for everyone, even the bluebirds, as long as the teachers were skilled and motivated.

New Haven Unified became among the first to implement heterogeneous classrooms in grades K – 8. Eventually, even the high school opened its honors and advanced placement classes to anyone willing to do the work, regardless of prerequisites.

The district also cored its history and Language Art classes, a powerful, synergistic combination that I gleefully taught for fourteen years. And we evaluated student reading and writing using truly authentic assessment (grading essays according to a rubric we'd created, for instance, instead of scanning a fill-in-the-bubble test), a method that held everyone accountable, students and teachers alike, as teachers graded the essays their colleagues' students had written.

Guy believed that, since New Haven was such an incredibly diverse district (the students spoke more than 25 different languages), equity was paramount. Which is why, as the district grew, he refused to build an additional high school, fearing that the two schools would become as segregated as the local community. He insisted on keeping everyone together at the same, strong school. And so, James Logan High became a behemoth of 4,200 students, its sprawling campus larger than most community colleges.

Logan was controversial. Its motto was "Diversity is our strength, unity our goal," but creating a real sense of community among such a large population remained a daunting challenge, and certainly more than a few at-risk students slipped through its cracks.

On the other hand, because of its size, Logan could offer an incredibly broad array of courses, electives and student clubs. Its sports teams, bands, and forensic program became state, sometimes even national champions.

The state superintendent cited New Haven as an exemplary district. Teams of educators came from far and wide to observe, to learn, to imitate.

Thus, Guy Emanuele and his team instilled everyone— staff, students and parents—with an ardent sense of achievement and pride. They proved, to borrow from Margaret Mead, "that a small group of thoughtful, committed citizens can change the world." They certainly changed the lives of thousands of New Haven families.

* * *

Even so, I am most grateful to Guy for what he did for the district's LGBTQ+ students and staff.

I had finally accepted myself as gay, but remained a frightened, closeted educator. My friend, Teri, was too. We were frustrated especially because we knew how badly our queer students suffered. We'd heard rumors that Guy might be gay-friendly, but knew he would soon to retire, closing our window of opportunity. Teri and I gulped, and made an appointment to see Guy.

On the way down the long hall to his office, I turned to Teri and said, "You know, we could just turn around and run away." Five minutes later, I took a big breath and uttered, "Guy, I'm gay and she's lesbian. We're both mentor teachers. We want to teach our colleagues how make their classrooms and schools safe for all kids, especially those like us."

We never could have imagined how our plea came to Guy like manna from Heaven.

You see, a neighborhood community group had recently announced the first-ever gay prom, which had made national headlines, and which had sparked a long-needed public discussion about why a separate prom might be necessary. The local press had published a story about a youth named Peter who'd dropped out of Logan because of all the harassment and bullying he'd endured.

The only thing Guy hated more than bad press was the thought of his district letting down a minority kid. He'd called Peter in for an hours-long interview. Afterward, at a BBQ he'd organized for administrators at his home, he'd exploded, "We are complicit in the torment, the drop-outs, even the suicides of these gay kids!" But, what to do?

Then, Teri and I miraculously appeared in his office.

Guy paved our way through the ensuing controversy. He met with each of the school board members to insist on their support. He called together his entire administrative team to let them know what Teri and I were undertaking. When one of the principals asked, "Oh, great. Now we have openly-gay teachers. What am I supposed to say when parents call demanding their kids be removed from 'that faggot's' classroom?" The associate superintendent replied tersely, "Well, what do you say now when a parent asks for a kid to be removed from 'that [African American's]' classroom?" When fundamentalist teachers protested, the board of education didn't blink; and Guy let them know there were plenty of other districts where they could work. When the conservative Rutherford Institute threatened to sue, Guy replied, "Bring it on." (The institute never did.)

Over the next two years, Teri and I conducted our "Invisible Minority" training in one district school after the next. We shared the special risks LGBTQ+ youths face—not just bullying and dropping out, but shocking rates of homelessness (parents kicking their gay kids out onto the streets), drug addiction, and suicide. We taught how to ensure that all classrooms became welcoming, inclusive places for everyone.

We culminated with a panel of gay youth, who always stole the show with their courage and their poignant, often heart-wrenching coming-out stories. Peter's anecdote has stayed with me: "Everyone hated me, so I hated myself. I wanted to believe there was a white picket fence in my future. But I didn't."

Most of our colleagues were horrified, moved, grateful, then finally inspired. (Guy insisted we repeat the "Invisible Minority" training every year for all new teachers.)

Afterward, Teri and I met with Guy again. "You support and protect us, but what about after you leave?" At Guy's insistence, the board immediately updated all non-discrimination policies to include LGBTQ+ students and staff. On a roll, we mentioned how unfair it was that, in the absence of gay marriage, our partners could not enjoy the same benefits as the spouses of married staff. Guy urged the board to expand district benefits to include all domestic partners.

And, just in case there were any doubts about how accepted LGBTQ+ teachers and students would be, Guy chose me to be district teacher of the year, and then promoted me to assistant principal. (Eventually, I even created an LGBTQ+ Studies class at Logan.)

Thus, almost overnight, Guy made New Haven, perhaps, the most progressive district in the nation.

It was a heady, exciting time, a golden age for both the district and me.

BARNARD-WHITE MIDDLE SCHOOL

Union City, California

My students drew an ugly effigy of me on the board, complete with horns, fangs, scars and earrings. One of them christened it with my new nickname, "Elly," which the most daring of them used flippantly instead of the more respectful "Mr. Ellison."

Later, during a writing lesson, when I'd urged everyone to always assume their reader was a stupid fool and so to explain really well, the kids added their own spin: Since I was usually their reader, they now responded to my pleas for elaborate writing with a gleeful "Because you're a stupid fool!"

That's when I knew it was going to be a good year. You see, junior high students typically express affection though such insults. And a classroom punctuated with easy laughter is a fun one, indeed—for me and my students.

I loved my job.

Consider the fact that I'd begun the year by teaching three stories by Latino author Gary Soto, then followed with another by Langston Hughes. When I grew up in Ohio, I read literature only by and about white people. And my history course covered only Europe. (Asia, Africa, and Latin America apparently had no history back then.) It gave me great pleasure and pride to know my colleagues and I usually taught better than we'd been taught ourselves.

Hughes' poignant story, "Thank You, M'am," told of a chance meeting on the streets of Harlem between a troubled teen purse-snatcher and his strong-willed intended victim—a scrappy woman who, with cunning, tough-love wisdom, taught the boy to respect himself. "Ain't you got nobody home to tell you to wash your face?" she asked just before putting him in a half nelson. "Then it will get washed this evening," and she dragged the hapless boy home to her apartment.

It occurred to me that my job as a teacher was to be just like that woman, to similarly drag my students kicking and screaming into taking pride in themselves—into carefully proofreading every assignment now; and, ultimately, into reaching for lofty goals for their future. I, too, demanded that kids "wash their faces."

It was a damned important job; and, even though I didn't always succeed, the attempt was both noble and fulfilling.

Also, no matter what the current President, governor or principal said, my classroom was still my kingdom. I decided what went on within its four walls. I could, tapping into my love of history, reading and writing, my wacky sense of humor, my flair for the dramatic, and my dogged belief that everyone could succeed, create magic there. (Provided, of course, I'd managed to get enough sleep and exercise.) It was a freedom/responsibility few other professionals ever knew.

One morning, I donned a sheet as a make-shift toga, and grandly recited Marc Antony's rebuttal to Brutus, "Friends, Romans, countrymen, lend me your ears!" Afterward, as I wandered the class, and beheld thirty-three adolescents struggling with their partners to make sense of Shakespeare's captivating text, I experienced a blessed moment of self-awareness, one I enjoy often as a teacher: Despite all the politics lurking outside my class, and even in spite of the depressing pile of uncorrected papers looming on my desk, there was no place on Earth I'd rather be.

But, of course, I was (am) a stupid fool.

* * *

"What the hell's the matter with you, Cindy? Don't you give a damn about anyone except yourself?"

Those angry words of mine would haunt me for the rest of the year, and color forever my relationship with one of my students, Cindy. I blurted them one day when my students were working on a project in teams. Cindy—clearly bright but ever caustic—had publicly humiliated a less-gifted, terribly shy boy on her team, and I'd called her back to my desk for a thorough dressing down. I was furious.

Soon, Cindy was too. Before the day had ended, she'd already complained to the principal about my outrageous profanity. She'd embellished her version a bit, though, substituting some other, more colorful four-letter words in place of "hell" and "damn."

To this day I bristle at the memory of the ensuing investigation, which involved the principal, two assistant principals, one parent, and three student witnesses. I was on the defensive, blushing, stammering, struggling to defend my reputation before my peers. Even though I finally proved I hadn't uttered the awful words Cindy'd claimed, I did have to apologize for the unwise ones I had. Meanwhile, Cindy apologized for nothing.

Afterward, noticing my lingering rage, the principal asked pointedly, "Dave, can you still teach Cindy? Perhaps I should move her to another class."

"No," I sighed after a few, pensive moments, "I lost my temper, and Cindy cunningly seized the opportunity to turn the tables. I deserved it. Besides, I have to grudgingly admire her. She really used her head. Now I'd like to teach her to use her heart as well. I'll be fine."

I wasn't, though. Oh, I kept my cool for the rest of the year, even in the face of Cindy's persistent, ugly defiance. I even complimented her insights often in class. But I kept my distance as well. While I was frivolously silly with other kids, I remained cautious, cold, professional in my interactions with Cindy. I told myself this was only prudent. In retrospect, I believe it was my form of subtle vengeance. I withheld from Cindy the warmth I lavished on others, and so hoped to exact a heavy price for having embarrassed me.

I succeeded. Cindy never smiled for the rest of the year.

On the last day of school, Cindy once again turned the tables. She waited after class, awkwardly thrust a small box into my hands, and then vanished out the door. Inside the box was beautiful tie.

I stared at it a long while. Was it a belated apology? Was it a thank-you for at least treating her with respect? Was it a futile attempt to buy back my affection? It didn't really matter, I suppose, because it was too late. The year was over. Cindy was gone.

I won't forget Cindy or our strained year together. I stubbornly waited for a young girl to ask my forgiveness. In the end, it was I who was sorry.

✳✳✳

Carlos could make it, despite himself. Of course, he'd have every excuse if he failed. He'd never known a father, and his mother had been brutally murdered in a drug deal down by the tracks. Now he lived with his grandparents who, although they loved him, didn't quite know what to do with him. As he grew older, they became more afraid. And so did he. Only thirteen, and yet, unwittingly, he faced such difficult, dangerous choices.

I remember Halloween when Carlos came to school dressed as a gang member. With dark glasses, a red bandanna and a penciled-in mustache, he played the role so well he startled me. Then I guessed—or, perhaps, only hoped—that his donning the costume was merely a queer, desperate attempt to distance himself from the role, to call it a masquerade, something fake he could discard with ease at any time.

Carlos wanted to escape the barrio. I often told him a good education was his way out, and I think he half believed me. Every now and again he'd turn in some impressive work just to reassure himself—and me?— that he really could do it. Yet, more often he shied away from academic success, fleeing that insidious label, "school boy," which would mean banishment from his friends. How could I—an adult, a *güero* (whitey)— speak more convincingly than they?

I thought for a time Carlos hated me. He peppered my lessons with arrogant defiance, playing Devil's Advocate with many ideas I expressed, nearly every instruction I gave. One afternoon, though, I witnessed him do the same with another teacher. When she took his bait and engaged him in an angry debate, I noticed his disappointment.

Thus, Carlos taught me I would never win an argument with him, or any adolescent for that matter. And, in his incessant attempts to tear me and other adults down, he finally revealed his dogged search for someone to respect. He'd never admit it, not even to himself, but perhaps he was hoping one of us would one day win.

That's why I began to counter so many of his "What for?'s" with a terse, "Because I'm mean and unreasonable. Now get to work!" I left him no reply.

He was shocked at first. Later he only mumbled beneath his breath. Nonetheless, class by class, he challenged less, seemed to listen more. And when, after one brief, particularly harsh rebuke I leaned down and whispered, "It's my hemorrhoids, Carlos. That's why I'm so bad," he actually smirked. What's more important, he did get to work.

Yes, I had high hopes for Carlos. Maybe he did for me, too.

71

* * *

My principal had just stepped out from the office, and stood stolidly on the raised patio like a ship's captain on her quarterdeck, surveying the students milling about the courtyard below. Her face furrowed into a frown, however, when a young girl ran past shrieking beneath her, pursued shortly afterward by the distraught student's teacher, strumming his guitar. He stopped, greeted the principal deferentially, then resumed the chase, serenading plaintively between gasps.

Shaking her head with bemused resignation, the principal retreated back to her office, mumbling, "Mr. Ellison, when will you ever grow up?"

I like to believe that my silliness is evidence that teaching middle school has kept me forever young. After all, I recall some long-lost study citing how much more often children laugh relative to somber adults; and Jesus' admonition that, if we want to enter Heaven, we must become like little children.

So, I've nurtured over the years a perpetual zaniness, manifested in, for example, my outlandish ties. (The Potato Head tie is my favorite.) And my practice of including ridiculous answers for quiz questions, such as this one on the Reformation: "Ellisonism," which matched with option D, "Belief that those predestined for Salvation can be recognized by their bald heads." (I'm bald.)

And my penchant for, when collecting assignments (especially important projects), sneezing raucously onto one of the papers, and using it to apparently wipe my nose.

And my bad habit of following closely behind students during lunch and endeavoring to step on their shoe's heel, thus giving them a "flat tire." That prank backfired, though, since soon a passel of kids followed me around campus attempting to return the favor.

I perpetrate another favorite shoe-hoax of mine whenever I come upon one of my students loitering outside my class with untied shoe laces. I step on one lace; then, with exaggerated severity, admonish the student to hustle in to class immediately. "I'm not going to ask you again, young man. Get to class! Now! Come on! No, I'm not interested in your excuses. Move along! Don't talk back to me! Get to class right now!" Soon a crowd of my students gathers grinning, and we're all late for class.

Such humor (or, attempts at it) run in the family. My older brother, Tim, for example, responds to any cashier's "Have a nice day!" with a deadpan, "I'm sorry, but I've made other plans."

Once my father responded with impatience, "Geez, Tim doesn't take anything seriously."

I informed him that, actually, it was quite the opposite: Tim, ever the existentialistic philosopher, took everything way too seriously; so much so that I often worried for him. His humor was his attempt to compensate, to survive. Abraham Lincoln was famous for doing the same during The Civil War.

Similarly, I'm fanatical about teaching, holding my students to extremely high standards for work and behavior. I'm often uncompromisingly strict. I hope my silliness enables my students to see that I'm still human and approachable. And it forces me to get down off my high horse every now and then, and laugh—mostly at myself.

Once, while passing out an assignment, I inadvertently missed one student. "You forgot me, Mr. Ellison," she called.

"No, I didn't," I responded with a deadpan to make my brother proud. "I just don't like you."

The next morning the same student failed to pass up her homework. To my inquisitive scowl she responded, "I didn't forget, Mr. Ellison. I just don't like you!"

Backfired again.

✳ ✳ ✳

How do you say goodbye to your best friend? Not the normal goodbye, such as when two teens might head off to different colleges, wishing each other luck. No, Deonte's friend, Steven, was dying. There would be no college for him, nor even, perhaps, a tomorrow. This would be no ordinary good-bye.

Of course, Steven was no ordinary friend. Deonte had met him in the first grade, and remained in the same class with him for the next five years. As they both matured, so did their friendship. They played baseball, football, and basketball together. In the school band, Steven played the trumpet, Deonte the drums. The two looked forward anxiously to the day when they'd finally don their uniforms, and go on tour with the varsity band.

Over the years, Deonte learned to depend on Steven. As bright as Deonte was, he tried the patience of many a principal, teacher, and coach, including me. He relied upon Steven's calming presence, his steady example to keep him on the straight and narrow.

Then the fickle hand of fate struck Steven with Leukemia.

Everyone clung to hope. There was chemotherapy, and maybe even a bone-marrow transplant. Steven would pull through. He just had to. After all, he was a straight-A student, winning all sorts of academic and service awards. Everybody liked him.

Leukemia, ever merciless, didn't take any of that into account. It continued its unrelenting ravage until, finally, Steven left the hospital for the last time. There was nothing more the doctors could do. Steven came home to die.

It was only then that Deonte accepted the awful fact that he'd have to say good-bye to Steven, forever. But how?

That evening, the entire band assembled in front of Steven's house. Many teachers, students and neighbors gathered as well, hugging and consoling each other, all struggling to maintain a strained smile for Steven.

He finally emerged, doped with morphine, confined to a wheel chair, sucking air through an oxygen mask. Nonetheless, his indomitable spirit had prevailed over his weakened body: he sported a broad smile, and the glittering band uniform he had always longed to wear. No wonder Deonte liked him so much!

How could Deonte play, tucked away in the back of the band with the rest of the drums? It just didn't seem enough. He needed Steven to see him, to hear him. So, quietly, he moved to the front, and stationed himself right next to Steven. The director, gave him a nod, and lifted his baton. Then the concert began.

And Deonte played for him, ba-rum-pa-pa-pum. The brass and winds kept time, ba-rum-pa-pa-pum. He played his drum for him ba-rum-pa-pa-pum. He played his best for him ba-rum-pa-pa-pum, rum-pa-pa-pum, rum-pa-pa-pum. He and his drum.

It was an incredibly beautiful, simple, profound gesture—one befitting the birth of a King, and the death of Deonte's best friend.

✳ ✳ ✳

I was haunted by three spirits.

I sat eating a bag-lunch in San Francisco's Union Square, marveling at the tallest Christmas tree I'd ever seen, while keeping a wary eye on my 8th graders as they gleefully romped from bench to bush to tree. Clearly our field trip to a production of Dickens' *A Christmas Carol* was a scintillating adventure for them, and for me. I rarely had such leisure to appreciate my students for the remarkable, unfathomable individuals they were.

Most of the kids gathered in small groups, as was their wont, betraying their various personalities and allegiances.

The sight of Adam standing alone, however, conjured up the unbidden ghost of some terrible Christmas past, which had left him scarred both physically and emotionally. Bright but unskilled, polite but ever-aloof, Adam worried me. So far I'd failed to help him, comprehend him, or even converse with him. So had everyone else.

Across the square, as unobtrusive as possible, sat Sylvia and Richard, together. Birds of a feather, I mused.

I'd called Sylvia's home just days before, only to discover that Mom lived elsewhere, Dad was on the road, and grandma was asleep. Apparently Sylvia would have to raise herself. We spoke for a bit about how she must learn to be more responsible, much more mature. She'd seemed flattered by our impromptu man-to-woman chat. But, would she finally do her work? Would she be able to resist the advances of the older high school boys next year, who'd mark her easy prey?

Richard, meanwhile, faced an awful choice himself. I'd asked him once, "How many of your friends in the gang earned a college degree? How many have so much as a high school diploma? Beware, Richard: You will become who your friends are. You're going to have to choose, the gang or an education." Such simplistic advice! I'd urged him to "just say no" to virtually everything, everyone he'd ever known. What kind of viable alternative could I provide?

There they sat, Sylvia and Richard, chatting innocently, oblivious to the dark specter of their future, fraught with peril.

A shout from one of my students startled me, dispelling my woeful reveries. I quickly glanced around the park where the other kids still frolicked with barely concealed wonder at all the exotic sights and discordant sounds of San Francisco, resplendent in its holiday finery. Even a Scrooge like me couldn't help but laugh along with them.

Before we left, I spied Adam edging his way towards a group of boys who were pestering some pigeons, and he joined shyly in their mischief.

Later, I looked back over at Sylvia and Richard. They did make an awfully cute couple. And hadn't they come together for tutoring last week?

So, the Spirit of Christmas Present won out in the end. Yes, the world's still often cruel to children, just as it was in Dickens' day. But there's still hope for them as well, and sometimes even joy.

Indeed, I finally led my students Pied-Piper-like along The City's bustling sidewalks to the theater, where Dickens had his magical way with them.

And, along with Tiny Tim, I prayed God would bless them, every one.

✳ ✳ ✳

"What a dweeb," Sammy mumbled just loudly enough for everyone in the class to hear. He'd been misbehaving all class, his insolence growing more brazen. This time he'd gone too far. No one calls me a dweeb!

I lunged for Sammy from behind the overhead projector, leaving it pointing crazily towards the side wall. I didn't care. Grabbing him forcefully by the collar of his open jacket, I jerked him violently out of his desk, sending it flying askew. "I'll show you what happens to awful students like you!" I roared. Then, trembling with rage, I dragged him headlong outside.

I imagine the entire hall heard the crash into the lockers, and then the wicked slap of my hand. Sammy gasped in shock and agony, but I showed no remorse. "Now get out of here, and never come back!"

I stormed back into the room, my face fuming, my lungs still heaving, and glared at the other students. "What?" I responded lamely to their incredulous, wide eyes.

"But, Mr. Ellison," one intrepid girl ventured, shaking her head, "you...can't. You...just can't do that."

"Why? This is my classroom! I'm in charge here! And I will never— Do you hear me?—I will never, ever tolerate such disrespect! Sammy deserved it. All of it!"

"That's against the law," a voice called out timidly from the back.

"Who said that?" I spat. "Who said that? I'll ask only once more: Who said that? Because," and then I finally gave way to the grin I'd only barely been able to stifle, "you're right."

After a dramatic moment of silence, I called out, "OK, Sammy, you can come back in now." And Sammy bounded back to his desk, his grin almost as wide as mine. "Thanks, Sammy."

Looking in wonder from him to me, the class let out a collective sigh of confusion, then relief, and finally amused annoyance. They realized they'd been had.

"Yes, you're right. Although I am in charge here, that was against the law. Even I have to obey the law. How many of you were going to tell your parents I slapped Sammy today?" Every hand went slowly up. "In fact, how many were going straight to the principal at recess?" All the hands stayed up.

"You see, you all understood intuitively the far-reaching and long-lasting results of something which occurred almost eight hundred years ago. When Richard the Lion Heart died, his inept brother, John, inherited the English throne. John was almost as bad as I am. He thought he could do whatever he wanted, mistreat and exploit his subjects however he willed.

"Finally the nobles had enough. In the year 1215 A.D., they cornered him in a field one day and, at the point of a sword, forced him to sign *The Magna Carta*. It was an amazing document which, for the first time since the fall of the Roman Republic, became a supreme law, above everyone, including King John. And ever since then, everybody—kings, presidents, even history teachers like me—have had to obey the law.

"You knew that. You just didn't know why. Or how it began. Or the profound debt you owe those brave nobles of so long ago.

So, today, let's find out who they were, what they accomplished, and why it's still so important. Open your texts to page 270.

"Oh, and one more thing," I added, massaging tenderly the welt on the back of my hand where I'd slapped myself. "For the record: I am not a dweeb!"

✳ ✳ ✳

Philip fulfilled a fantasy of mine. Unlike him, I'd been a puny eighth-grader, the scrawny kid the bullies loved to pick on. I always imagined that one day I would learn Jujitsu or Karate, and take my revenge.

More recently, I'd fantasized that a monster of a student, such as huge football player, would advance upon me in class, backing me into a corner. With the rest of my students staring wide-eyed, I would vanquish him with a single "Hai-ya!" and he would crumble to the floor. Of course, the best part would be the looks of awe I would enjoy afterward as I walked through the halls.

I never imagined that the monster would be as nice as Philip.

I came to know Philip because two of my students were his only friends. The three of them would often harass me during recess in a good-natured, junior-high sort of way. They traded bald jokes, each one trying to out-do the other. "Oh, Mr. Ellison, please wear a hat! The glare off your head is blinding me!" Philip, on the other hand, stayed with one, consistent prank. Towering above me, he mimicked the sound of spitting, and then pantomimed the motions of buffing and shining the top of my head. I feigned impatience with it all. But, to be honest, Philip and his friends made me laugh.

One day when Philip came to my classroom, I needed to talk with his two friends privately. I asked him to wait outside. On his way out, he attacked another student, whom he would have pummeled to pieces had I not intervened. I grabbed Philip in a bear hug, pinning his arms. Nonetheless, he continued to struggle hysterically. I finally just fell to the floor, bringing him with me. Stunned, he lay there motionless until the assistant principal arrived.

Only after I spoke to the counselor did I understand what had happened. For the past several months Philip's mother had abandoned Philip for her new boyfriend. She no longer cooked or cleaned for him. In fact, she seemed to have completely forgotten about him, leaving him alone to raise himself. I could imagine the rejection and the anger he must have felt. Then, when I appeared to exclude him from his only friends, he snapped. He lashed out at the first student who looked at him the wrong way.

Later, I saw Philip crying alone in the assistant principal's office. He wasn't the monster of my fantasy. He was merely a confused, hurt, lonely boy.

On my way back to class, many students gathered around me to ask, "Is it true you 'slammed' Philip?" News of a fight travels fast in a middle school. Even the Gym teacher clenched his fist as I passed, and saluted me with a new nickname, "Hammer Man!" How often had I wished for just such a reputation? Now I couldn't stand it, knowing I had earned it at Philip's expense.

I forbade anyone to use the nickname or to even mention the fight. And I waited anxiously for Philip's return, hoping against hope he'd still want to give my head a buff and a shine.

✳ ✳ ✳

"Mr. Ellison, what does rainbow mean?" asked Priscilla.

I'd anticipated such a question since I wore a Rainbow Pride bracelet. I'd felt that I had a moral and professional responsibility to be "out" to my students, to be the role model I'd never had. My principal and superintendent had agreed.

Even so, I needed to walk a fine line in order to avoid the charge of using my classroom "to promote the gay agenda." And, no matter how careful I was, how would parents respond? How would my students?

"Let's stay focused on today's lesson," I replied. "I'll be happy to answer that question after class if you really want to know."

Priscilla, a bright, spunky, tenacious girl, returned after school with her entourage. "OK, will you answer me now? What does rainbow mean?"

"Gay pride," I answered as nonchalantly as I could.

"Does that mean you're gay?"

"Yes, of course."

"Cool," was all she said.

But, little Paco, who was doodling on the white board next to my desk, responded the most remarkably. Without even looking up from his drawing, he remarked, "You know, Mr. E, I'm really proud of you for being proud of yourself." For a while, that was the end of the discussion.

Of course, there was the afternoon when we were learning about Richard the Lionheart and his mother's, Eleanor of Aquitaine's, frustrated attempts to get him to marry, to provide the kingdom an heir. Why was he so reluctant? "Well, let's just say Richard and I may have at least one thing in common," I explained. My students looked confused, then twisted their heads and eyes to one side as they understood, murmuring, "Ah."

Anyway, I was finally out to my students, and, to my surprise and relief, this turned out to be no big deal, as an anecdote the assistant principal later shared with me made humorously clear. He'd been supervising the cafeteria during lunch, wandering among the tables eavesdropping on the kids' conversations. At one table, a student announced, "Hey, you know, Mr. Ellison is gay." "Yeah, so what?" another kid replied. "But, did you hear? He doesn't own a TV!" Now that was beyond the pale.

Some of the parents weren't thrilled with my being openly gay; yet, as one later remarked dryly, "Oh, Mr. E, that was just one more outrageous story coming home from your class which dominated our dinner table conversations."

So, my being gay never became the issue I feared.

At least, not until Jason arrived. Jason had been in a Special Education class for kids with significant learning disabilities. But, he'd improved so much that his teacher, counselor, and parents had decided to try him in a mainstream classroom, choosing mine.

Normally, I'd be thrilled. The trouble was, Jason was such an adorably cute young man, with dimples and gigantic eyelashes. In fact, the morning he arrived, the special education aide came over and whispered, "My, that Jason is a looker, isn't he?"

"I'm not supposed to notice such things."

"Well, let me tell 'ya!" she replied with a laugh.

And now I, Jason's openly gay teacher, was going to have to shower him with a lot of special attention. What would the other students think?

Things turned out far worse than I feared. The second day, for example, Jason interrupted a lesson to ask, "What does rainbow mean?" The other kids just rolled their eyes.

"Mike, would you fill Jason in during lunch today," I replied lamely.

The next day, "Where did you get that rainbow bracelet, Mr. E? 'Cause I'd like one."

Oh boy.

Another day, when I squatted down next to Jason's desk to explain a difficult task, pointing to a line in his text, Jason reached out and began to play with the hair on my arm. I jerked it back, aghast.

Oh boy. Oh boy.

Just before lunch that day, Jason came to me with another question, this time placing his hand on my shoulder. "Jason, you need to take your hand off my shoulder."

"Why?"

"It's not appropriate for you to touch me, Jason," I said, removing his hand. I was losing my mind. How would this end?

But it did, gracefully, moments later when the bell for lunch rang. Pricilla tarried, waiting until the class was empty except for the two of us. She'd noticed everything, especially my exasperated terror. "Mr. E, you need to relax," she stated matter-of-factly. "Jason just has a crush on you." She shrugged her shoulders, then left.

From the mouths of babes....

***

I saved the best for last, a hundred-and-one year-old epic poem, Alfred Noyes' "The Highwayman."

First, I played singer Loreena McKennitt's musical rendition, and watched bemused while my students rolled their eyes at each other. By the third stanza, though, the poem's powerful rhythm and McKennitt's haunting voice began their magic, and the kids' gaze fell inexorably to the text, searching for the rich themes I'd promised: love, crime, betrayal, sex, sacrifice, revenge, death, and ghosts....

After the first time through, my students still didn't grasp the plot; but they'd understood enough phrases—"Watch for me by moonlight.... There was death at every window.... Drenched in her own red blood.... They shot him down on the highway...."—to recognize a great yarn lay buried, waiting for them to uncover it. They were intrigued.

We started with the first stanza, which set an eerie scene with its memorable metaphors: "The wind was a torrent of darkness among the gusty trees; the moon was a ghostly galleon tossed upon cloudy seas; the road was a ribbon of moonlight over the purple moor; and the highwayman came riding, riding, riding.... up to the old inn door."

A professor of mine once commented that poetry teaches us how to see; and I know my students were learning anew how to hear a night wind, how to see the night sky.

The highwayman galloped into the second stanza with his imported French hat, his fancy velvet coat, his frilly shirt, his jeweled sword. "He's styling!" one student summarized. "Man, he is fine," agreed another. "No wonder the landlord's daughter fell for him." "Oh, he thinks he's all that," complained a boy. "Maybe he is!" retorted another. And, without my prompting, the students continued to make inferences: "He must be a good thief." "Then, why does he keep stealing?"

Later, as the ruthless Redcoats tied the landlord's black-eyed daughter to her bed "with many a sniggering jest," using her as the bait to lure the highwayman to his death, the students recognized the sexual innuendos, realized they'd graduated to adult texts, and they were hooked.

When "her musket shattered the moonlight, shattered her breast in the moonlight and warned him—with her death," the students remained silent, savoring the tragedy, the melodrama, even the metaphor.

But when, enraged, the Highwayman returned the next morning, "Back he spurred like a madman, shrieking a curse to the sky, with the white road smoking behind him, and his rapier brandished high," the students erupted: "How stupid! He threw his life away!" "Well, what do you expect? He loved her!" "He wanted revenge." "Maybe he wanted to die…."

As I pointed out the irony in the line "And he lay in his blood on the highway, with the bunch of lace at his throat," the kids found a grim satisfaction with it.

When I asked if Loreena McKennitt had got the meter right in singing one phrase, the students joined me in clapping out the rhythm. No, McKennitt had got it wrong…and I chuckled inwardly as many shook their heads in annoyance: Weren't these the same kids who'd, just a few days before, rolled their eyes at this poem?

CALIFORNIA STATE UNIVERSITY, EAST BAY

Hayward, California

For five years, I co-taught the Social Studies Methods course for new teachers at Cal. State East Bay. I'd invited a program graduate to return and speak who had, after only three years in the trenches of Oakland's schools, already founded his own charter school.

I'll call him Che, because, like the Latin-American revolutionary, Ernesto "Che" Guevarra, he'd evinced uncommon ability and passion, even as a student-teacher. "Urban schools are designed to fail their students," he'd claimed. "They're part of a conspiracy of the ruling white oligarchy to keep minorities down." It was no surprise when Che soon became fed up with the middle school where he first taught. It was remarkable, though, when he recruited five like-minded colleagues to help him start an alternative school just a few blocks away.

Che and his young faculty worked with a dedication that left me dumbfounded. They spent their summers educating neighborhood families about the charter school, inviting one and all to enroll (except, as with most charter schools, any special education students or those not fluent in English), but making it clear that every parent and every child would have to adhere to a strict contract of responsibilities.

During the school year, Che and his zealous teachers labored more than twelve hours a day to ensure each child both faced rigorous challenges and received enough individualized support to meet them. Putting into practice Paulo Freire's *Pedagogy of the Oppressed*, they endeavored not just to teach students academic knowledge and skill, but to transform their image of themselves and the world.

Thus, Che created an almost unimaginable oasis of hope for some of Oakland's apparently hopeless children.

I doubted, however, that Che's vision would be sustainable, much less replicable. For instance, could he and his staff continue to make their school the center of their lives even as they grew older, perhaps fell in love and created families and children of their own? (In fact, most charter schools burn their typically young teachers out in just four years—replacing them with other new ones, thus keeping their costs artificially low.) But, what an inspiring speaker Che would be for the new teachers in my class!

Or, so I'd thought. Once Che finished his presentation, one of those teachers raised a hand to respond, his voice tremulous with fury: "I'm really happy to hear you and your school are doing so well. But I just started teaching at your former school. What the hell are my colleagues and I supposed to do now that you've lured away most of our best teachers, strongest students, and involved parents? The children you left behind, my students, are no less deserving than yours. What do you have to say to them who now languish in the school your charter devastated? What do you have to say to me? Should I, too, abandon them and my school?"

After a stunned silence, Che replied only that he'd given up on Oakland's public schools and so had attempted to save at least a few kids from them.

The road to Hell is paved with good intentions.

ASSISTANT PRINCIPAL

Barnard-White Middle School, Union City, California
Willard Junior High School, Berkeley, California

The custodian found the empty beer can in the boys' restroom the third day of school in late August.

Being a new middle school vice principal at the time, I merely shrugged my shoulders, and sighed, "Well, what can we do?"

"A lot," Ms. Gold, the principal, replied. "This is when and where we draw the line."

She threw out her dragnet, interviewing the custodian to determine after which recess the can had appeared; and then the teachers on supervision to discover which boys frequented the restroom at that time. Because she knew all the kids so well, she could pretty well guess which ones had been involved, and who had been their ringleader.

"Tony," Ms. Gold concluded with grim certainty.

The short drama began in her office moments later, which she staged artfully. She sat behind her desk, placing me and the other vice principal, Miss Soto, on either side of the "hot seat" in front of her. "Ready?" she quipped to Miss Soto, who nodded.

In came Tony, looking startled to see the entire administrative team there in the office confronting him. After a long moment of silence, Ms. Gold began: "So, Tony, how's it going?"

He gulped and replied with a pubescent squeak, "Fine."

"That's good, Tony," she replied. "Very good. So, is there anything you want to tell me?"

"No."

"Really?" Ms. Gold continued staring at Tony fixedly, her relentless eyes a perfect counterpoint to her small, cat-bird-seat smile. "Nothing about the beer on campus yesterday?"

He shook his head convincingly.

"Oh? Nothing about the can on the floor of the boys' restroom during morning recess?" she continued, looking briefly at the paper on her clipboard (which I knew was merely the day's lunch menu).

"No."

"Hmmm. That's odd. Because Mrs. Thompson observed you, Freddie, Javier, James…" she continued naming all his friends slowly, consulting the clipboard, "entering that restroom during morning recess."

Silence.

"Mrs. Thompson said, Tony, that you all were in there a very long time." Ms. Gold had made that part up. Still, her eyes and voice were both now icy cold and hard, her smile long gone.

Another silence dragged on excruciatingly.

Finally, Miss Soto, seated to the left of Tony, administered the *coup de grace*. With her soft, sweet voice she asked, "Where'd you find it, Tony?"

He turned to her and blurted out frantically, "Under a bush!" (The mythical bush where students claimed they found all contraband.)

"You fool!" I'd wanted to blurt out. "All you had to do was keep your mouth shut!"

"Thank you, Tony," Ms. Gold replied. Then she discussed with him—sternly, yet with obvious affection—why bringing the beer can to school had been so harmful to the school, to his friends, to himself and all his goals for the new year, Tony having shared them during their intimate conversation. "Well, Tony, I'm going to let it go, this time," she finished. "But there can't be another, no matter who brings it. You understand? Can I count on you?"

Tony nodded gratefully, and with a gushing "Thank you, Ms. Gold," he fled back to class.

"Why didn't you suspend him?" I asked, incredulous.

"David, there's policy, and there's what's best for Tony and this school," Ms. Gold explained patiently. "Tony gets into trouble frequently. If I suspended him now and got his year off on such a bad foot, I'd probably end up expelling him before the end of the year. Also, he is the leader of the 8th grade, for better or worse. I'd like to teach him to be a positive one. He owes me now, and so will be far more likely to be with us than against us. I do have high hopes for him, despite his awful home. "What is more, word will spread. By lunch today everyone in the 8th grade will know that a kid brought a beer to school and we'd tracked him down the very next morning. I like that.

"This is how we try to run this school, David. Not with an iron fist, but with a strong but loving hand. And that's the kind of hand I want you to use as my new assistant principal."

* * *

The call from the pool came just before recess. I grabbed my walkie-talkie and headed out the door of my office. A student had injured himself on the diving board during Physical Education Class.

Trying not to run, I hastened to the pool where I found a giant of an 8th grader sitting on the side of the pool, rocking himself back and forth, dangling one leg into the water, bellowing obscenities. One glance at his ankle and I knew it was fractured severely.

"I'm here, Freddie," I soothed, putting one arm around his shoulder. With the other I held up the walkie-talkie, instructing the office to dial 911, send down Freddie's emergency form, call his parents....

Freddie. My pet name for him was "Bubba," as he towered over me, and hefted at least 200 pounds. He and his friends had hung around my office most days after school, making themselves a welcome nuisance.

Nonetheless, I'd suspended the lot of them the previous week for tossing some firecrackers at an elderly volunteer tutor. Even more maddening was the fact that, afterward, they'd remained unrepentant in my office, lying and laughing about the whole escapade. I'd added an extra day of suspension for the ugly defiance, but had wondered since if I'd been motivated most by my feeling of betrayal. After the suspension, Freddie had avoided my office, and that had been fine by me.

All that was forgotten now. I called for some towels and covered Freddie's back. I debated if I should get him to lie down, elevate that ankle, try to prevent shock. But his steady stream of loud profanity deterred me. Before I knew it, the EMTs had arrived and pulled me gently away.

"Where're my things?" gasped Freddie wildly as the EMTs wrestled his stretcher into the ambulance.

"Up in front with me, Freddie," I assured him. Then I took my place next to the driver, feeling guilty about my excitement. I'd never ridden in an ambulance before. The driver attempted to make small talk while I cast worried glances back towards Freddie.

At the hospital there was no emergency room available, so Freddie moaned on his gurney in the middle of the corridor. I grasped his hand while nurses periodically took the pulse of his ankle, ensuring the fracture hadn't cut off the blood to his foot and toes.

At one awful moment, an aide rushed by recklessly and bumped the injured ankle. Freddie's prolonged shrieks brought curious heads peeking out from doors on either side of the busy hallway.

I squeezed his hand even more tightly, and aggressively mopped the sweat off his brow, hoping to distract him from the agony. "Take big breaths, Freddie. That's it. You're OK, Freddie. You're going to be OK...."

Finally his screaming subsided, and his eyes focused again. He stared for a moment at the fluorescent lights in the ceiling, then turned his head and looked at me.

And that's when he said it. Lying prostrate in the middle of the emergency ward, orderlies passing back and forth on either side of him, enduring excruciating pain, Freddie murmured, "Mr. Ellison, I sure am sorry about those fire crackers."

"That's alright, Freddie," I responded, stifling a laugh.

Kids never fail to amaze me.

***

"Willie organized an after-school balloon-toss game," I read on the disciplinary referral to my office, "using condoms instead of balloons."

Yet again I found myself struggling to maintain a stern face in response to Willie's silly antics. I looked up and inquired with feigned exasperation, "What am I going to do with you, Willie?"

"Adopt me?" he responded, his mirthful eyes betraying his deadpan delivery.

The truth is, I would have liked to. Willie swaggered zoot-suit style through the halls every day, his arms flailing with exaggerated gestures, and his ever-active mouth set in a wide grin. It was a desperate façade, I knew, given his learning disability and dismal home; but he still made me laugh, and had gladdened my heart with his newfound academic success.

Rob deserved the credit. A mentor from U.C. Berkeley, Rob had taken Willie under his wing four years before, assuming all the responsibilities and love Willie's parents never had. He'd attended

Willie's special education meetings, conferenced frequently with his teachers, tutored him after school, arranged for an inter-district transfer when Willie's drunken dad had abruptly moved, and had even taken Willie to an occasional A's game. Rob was an angel. (I'd have adopted him, too!) He'd inspired Willie to finally maintain B's in nearly all his classes. And he'd inspired me to believe, at least for while, that public schools, too, could succeed, even with at risk kids like Willie.

Then it all nearly came tumbling down. One morning my principal called me to her office with the news Willie would have to leave. The Berkeley superintendent was in the middle of a bitter teacher-contract dispute; and, as an apparent cost-cutting measure, he'd ordered the suspension of all inter-district transfers for special education students.

"You know Willie will never go to his local school," I spat. "This won't save the district one red cent. But it will destroy all we've done for Willie, all he's accomplished for himself. I won't make him a political sacrificial lamb. I won't do it!" And I stormed out.

Two days later, the principal handed me a superintendent's memo admonishing me to do my job. "Willie goes," she ordered. "Today."

Rob's eyes flashed with hate when I told him, but he said nothing. Willie, too, was speechless. He just sat next to my desk, hugging himself, choking with sobs.

I called an emergency, secret meeting of Willie's teachers after school. "We could rewrite Willie's instructional education plan, exiting him from special education," one proffered. It would be a bogus, illegal document we'd all have to sign. It would fool no one. "Let's keep that as a last resort," I answered bleakly.

In the end, it was Rob who saved the day—again. He tracked down one of Willie's distant relatives who lived near school, and convinced her to put Willie up on the couch for the rest of the year.

So, Willie returned, once again ensconced behind his nonchalant façade, Rob's hand firmly on his shoulder. Despite the three-week hiatus in his education, he proved amazingly resilient, quickly catching up in all his classes—and with his inane referrals to my office.

* * *

Not so long ago, in a school not very far away, there was a vice principal named Mr. Ellison.

One morning, he stepped into a classroom, grateful to have escaped his office for a few moments. "Don't mind me," he whispered to Miss Jones at the door. "Just pretend I'm not here." Wearing creased Dockers, a collared shirt with a bright tie, Ellison looked every bit the administrator as he sat in the back with his clipboard.

He scanned the classroom walls, noting with displeasure that many of them were bare. Only one contained student-made charts stapled carelessly askew. The classroom arrangement was even worse, with the kids' desks strewn haphazardly. Ellison's frown deepened.

Some of the students looked over at him quizzically. Most of them in that upper-level math class had never graced his office, and so knew him only as the AP with the shiny bald head who wandered the field during lunch, supervising them at play, picking up trash, tossing off silly jokes as he went. Now, however, he looked so serious. They glanced nervously from him to Miss Jones.

Ellison jotted down another black mark because the kids were chatting amiably, not engaging in any sort of quiet warm-up activity before the class began. Didn't Miss Jones know even the basics of classroom management?

He now focused his gaze on Miss Jones, herself. She wore tennis shoes, faded jeans with a rip in one knee, and a wrinkled old t-shirt. "SLOVENLY," Ellison wrote in dark capital letters, already composing his scathing class observation (conveniently forgetting his own first years as a teacher). Then, to his horror, Miss Jones sat down cross-legged on her own desk before calling the class to attention. Who hired this woman?

"Hard or easy?" she asked.

"Hard!" the class moaned in unison.

"OK, let's see how you did." And with that, she left her desk and began wandering the room while her students quickly took out a long, mimeographed homework problem with their work below, and then moved into apparently random groups of various sizes—pairs, triads, quads, and even two groups of six. One group called out to a student in another, who laughed and then slid her chair over. What was this, the Red-Rover-Red-Rover approach to group design? Could this class possibly get any worse?

On the other hand, no more than a minute later, all the groups were busy at work. In fact, Ellison couldn't find a single student off-task. He stood up and strolled from group to group, eavesdropping.

"I got stuck here," he heard. "I did it another way." "You and I did it the same way, but got different answers. One of us is wrong! Maybe both. Ha!" "Oh my God, I see it now. How could I have been so stupid last night?"

Interesting, Ellison noticed, every single kid did the homework.

Ten minutes later, Ms. Jones called for attention, complimented the students for their efforts, and then chose three of them to put their homework on the board.

"But I got it wrong!" one complained.

"I know," Miss Jones replied. "But your approach was so clever. I think together we can fix it."

What followed was a raucous discussion of three different strategies for the same complicated problem, the kids debating the merits and pitfalls of each, eagerly calling out observations and questions, some rushing to the board to point, erase or add steps…. Miss Jones just stood in the back, occasionally tossing out praise or pointed questions. The students did most of the talking, though—to each other.

Ellison realized with embarrassment that his mouth was agape. He closed it into a smile.

"This is not a math class," his whispered to Ms. Jones on his way out the door. "It's a math club—student-centered, challenging, and fun. It's an amazing achievement."

Later, as he headed back to his office whistling softly, Ellison thought to himself, "Maybe I won't wear a tie tomorrow." And he lived happily ever after.

✳ ✳ ✳

Life had been unkind to Michael, and I did my best to take care of him. In the end, though, I only sent him on his way to his doom. That was my job.

Michael frequented my office mostly for silly, passive-aggressive types of misbehavior. He'd lose his textbook, again. Or chew gum, again. Or arrive tardy, call out a joke, not dress for gym, cut class, skip detention—again and again. He was always honest, uncommonly polite, but ever in trouble. I counseled him often, but to no avail.

All was explained during one of Michael's suspensions for smoking marijuana out behind the gym. His dad stormed into my office with, "I am so fed up with you, Michael! Why don't you just commit suicide?"

The only person his estranged parents treated more poorly than each other was Michael. They were profoundly bitter, ugly human beings, who took their unhappiness out on him.

Which only made me like and worry about him even more.

Finally, Michael found himself a really nice girlfriend, Tina, a quiet, studious angel who, like me, saw the goodness in him, and seemed to provide the warmth and affection he could find nowhere else. Just seeing them together made me glad.

Then, one day during recess I observed Michael look around furtively, slip something to Tina, who nodded while surreptitiously hiding it in her blouse.

No! No! No!

I confided in the other assistant principal, Ms. Soto, who just responded sullenly, "You need to do your job, Dave."

Immediately after recess, I went to Tina's classroom, escorted her to my office, and then asked her to give me what she'd hidden beneath her blouse. She obediently produced the marijuana, but refused to implicate Michael.

I knew what I had to do next, too. I brought Michael from class to another room. "I'm suspending Tina for the marijuana," I explained to him. "I know you gave it to her, but can't prove it. If you keep your mouth shut, you'll be fine. If you own up to it, however, given your record, I'd have to expel you."

"The marijuana was mine," Michael admitted without hesitation. "It's not her fault."

"I knew you'd say that," I choked. "Oh, I'm going to miss you, Michael!"

While I filled out the paperwork, I hastily gave him what I'd hoped would be useful parting advice: How, in spite of the expulsion, he should remember he was a good person. How I knew he could be a fine student. How, if he tried, he could still build for himself a happy life. How he deserved no less....

I never saw Michael again. Two years later his mother shot and killed her husband, Michael, and herself. I couldn't bring myself to his funeral. It was just too much.

In our society, we look to public schools to save our disadvantaged children—from broken homes, from poverty, ignorance, depression, gangs, drugs, injustice...everything. And I went into education hoping to do so.

I couldn't save Michael, though. My job was to protect the fortunate kids from him.

And there are so many Michaels.

KITAYAMA ELEMENTARY SCHOOL

Union City, California
(Back in the classroom where I belonged.)

O mar came to my attention after the first writing sample of the year in my new 4th grade class. His paragraph was nearly indecipherable, with his horribly misspelled words only barely held together with scant punctuation. He spoke English perfectly, even though Spanish was his native tongue; but he'd evidently done very little reading or writing in either language.

Helping Omar through our first book after school, a second-grade version of "The Three Pigs," had been grueling. He'd been unable to sound out even simple words like "straw," "brick," and "house." The situation seemed hopeless.

Nonetheless, he'd returned later in the week to read most of the story effortlessly, even with playful, dramatic expression. He'd beamed when, astounded, I'd showered him with praise.

"Well, I read the story six times," he explained.

"Wonderful!" I answered. "Let's go find you another book."

Moments later, we were both seated cross-legged on the floor of the library between the shelves, making our way through a more difficult but far more interesting text about an African-American girl on her first bus trip to town alone. She'd had to stand in the back despite the many open seats up front.

Omar listened to my explanation of the Jim Crow laws with horror, then eagerly turned the page. I paused and realized I was witnessing the magical moment when a youngster first glimpsed the power and joy of reading, the universe waiting just around the next page. I hadn't been a reading expert. I'd merely given him some one-on-one attention and guidance. And he'd blossomed!

Reality came crashing down soon enough. I started helping other struggling students after school as well, and so could no longer tutor Omar much. I tried pairing him up with another kid to read together, but that hadn't been as effective. Thus, both Omar and I recognized just how long and hard his road to real literacy would be.

My math class disillusioned me as well. I'd hoped the kids, working with their partners, would correct their homework in ten minutes or so. Forty minutes later I found myself unsuccessfully stifling frustration while answering the same question yet again, the kids still not finished, some of them barely having started.

Nancy, an identified Gifted and Talented student who sat in back, finally could stand it no more. She lay her head down on the desk, bored out of her mind. Normally, I'd call such a student back to attention. However, I thought to myself with sickening angst, "She's making better use of her time than I am," and let her nap.

Omar and Nancy in the same class, with such different needs…and I was failing them both.

I did my best to plan a better lesson for the following day. Even so, I went home utterly defeated. And since I didn't sleep well that evening, I returned the next morning still exhausted, still doubting my ability to teach at this new grade level, oblivious to the beauty of the day.

Then little Tania bounced into class long before the first bell, and came directly to my desk. I swiveled around in my chair to behold her face of boundless energy and enthusiasm, simple trust and joy. She hadn't noticed how awful a teacher I'd been the day before. No, she couldn't wait to make me laugh again.

She did within seconds, and so dispelled all my depression and doubt. In their place she left only gratitude. After all, my job was to nurture as best I could thirty-three such tiny, diverse, fragile yet resilient bundles of life and hope.

They all have that same amazing power over me—not only to make me laugh, but to make me believe in myself, in them, and in life.

Six million pounds of garbage: Alameda County's refuse for just one day, all collected in a huge, horrifying pit.

My class stood transfixed on a steel bridge above it, our mouths agape despite the awful stench. An endless stream of trucks backed to the pit's edge, dumping yet more tons onto the bizarre morass. Meanwhile, a giant bulldozer clawed to and fro below like some crazed beetle, oblivious to the trash bags and even furniture caught up in its massive treads. The dozer raced amid the quagmire to level the various heaps before the next truck made its dump.

"Who'd want that job?" one student asked.

"Do your homework," I replied.

My students and I were at Waste Management Incorporated's Davis Street Transfer Station in San Leandro. We were on an all-expense-paid Irecycle field trip for 4th and 5th graders sponsored by StopWaste.Org.

"They, too, want to 'get you while you're young,'" I'd explained to the kids. It was Red Ribbon Week, and we'd already discussed how tobacco companies had targeted children since the earlier a person becomes addicted to nicotine, the harder it is to ever quit. "The difference is, the instructors at StopWaste.Org aren't trying to hurt you or take your money. They're hoping to nurture both you and the Earth."

Alameda County has committed to reducing 75% of its waste. What better way to achieve such a noble goal than to change the minds, hearts and habits of young people (who might also nag their parents into finally doing the right thing at home)? It's a shrewd strategy, an all-too-rare example of a government taking the long view by investing in children.

StopWaste.Org teaches the Four Rs: Reduce, Reuse, Recycle, and Rot (compost). My students and I had discussed them the week before in class utilizing lessons StopWaste.Org had provided. And on the field trip itself we'd reviewed the 4 Rs in a much more hands-on fashion at the Irecycle School Education Center, right on the grounds of the transfer station.

Then, in a masterful lesson every educator would admire, we'd broken into small groups, each with its own fascinating bin, to simulate the sorting of recyclables taking place in the adjacent Materials Recovery Facility.

After donning protective glasses as well as bright yellow helmets and vests, we headed out like an incongruous line of tiny ducklings to wade through the frenetic transfer station. We passed by an enormous bale of 53,000 aluminum cans (which the kids now knew came from Bauxite) weighing a ton (which the kids pretended to remember was 2,000 pounds), able to be recycled into 180 bicycle frames. Other fun facts the kids found fascinating: glass comes from sand, and worm poop is good for plants!

Finally, we climbed above the massive pit of ever-growing putrefying trash. It could have been a scene from Dante's Inferno. Prompted by the instructors, the kids easily pointed out many, many objects that didn't belong in the pit—such as lumber, cardboard boxes, and plastic bottles—since such waste could have so easily been recycled. If only people had cared.

"Where does it all go?" one child asked as we debriefed afterward back in the Education Center.

"To the Altamont Landfill in Livermore, more than 2,000 football fields in size, 300 feet deep" one of the instructors, replied. "And it's already more than half full. Do you understand, kids, how important it is to practice the 4 Rs every day?"

My students nodded solemnly.

"We hope kids will make the connection between their daily choices and their impact on the environment," the other instructor explained to me as we departed.

Well, beholding six million pounds of teeming garbage was an uncommonly powerful lesson in consequences—one I, too, hope my students never forget.

***

Right when my 4th graders got off the bus at Fremont's Coyote Hills Regional Park, they'd sensed that here, amid marsh, trees and hills, they'd be on a longer leash, and so began chasing each other pointlessly, glorying in their rare freedom.

The kids calmed down obediently to work in teams on the scavenger hunt through the visitor center's many displays of Native Ohlone culture, including a full-size boat made of tule reeds and artistic baskets woven so tightly they held water. Later they toured the Ohlone Native village— sacred ground—crawling into a sweat lodge where the ranger held them captive with a spell-binding Ohlone myth. Next, they competed to see who could launch a spear the farthest using a Native tool, an *atlatl*.

After lunch, however, when the kids had completed their homemade kites, their running resumed. Who needed wind when they could sprint around? Who cared if some of the kites didn't fly well? The kids just ran harder.

Johnny added his own twist: While attempting to launch his kite, he'd tripped, but immediately decided that falling was at least half the fun. He ran around the shaded picnic area towing his kite, frequently finding some excuse to tumble to the ground, laughing only to himself.

The most exciting part of the day occurred late in the afternoon when I led everyone up Glider Hill Trail.

"Can I run on ahead, Mr. Ellison?" begged Amanjit.

I looked up to the summit and did my best to suppress a smirk. Poor Amanjit! He didn't understand how the steep incline would tucker him out in a matter of meters, and the rest of the class and I'd come upon him hunched over, heaving, humbled. Well, he'd learn soon enough. "Sure, go ahead."

Gleeful, Amanjit sprinted on and up. Then, like the Energizer Bunny, he just kept going and going.... I marveled when he reached the top without slowing. I became concerned when he continued, bounding gazelle-like along the ridge towards the companion summit. "Stop, Amanjit! Wait for the rest of us!" But he was already far out of my voice range—and, therefore, my control and protection. What kind of teacher was I?

Once on top, when my students beheld San Francisco Bay sparkling below, and the panorama of hills, bridges, cities and even mountains in the distance, they gasped in wonder and joy.

Unable to contain themselves, the same children who had only moments ago accused me of child abuse for dragging them up the steep trail began to tear pell-mell in all directions. It was a spectacle!

Amanjit led one group down a shoulder of the ridge towards a lower summit closer to the water. "Fools!" I mumbled. "They're going to have to hike all the way back up here." Even so, many other kids soon followed. "Eeeks!" I gasped when they disappeared beyond the other summit. I sprinted down after them.

It was a great field trip. Not only had my students learned a great deal about the Ohlone who once thrived in the Bay Area, but they'd behaved exactly the way I suspect Native children had, who'd spent most of their days outside, running these same hills.

On the way back down the trail towards the bus waiting in the parking lot below, the kids finally stopped running. One student tarried more than most, soon falling back to the end of the line with me.

"What's wrong, Maria? Are you OK?"
She turned and sighed ruefully, "I just don't want today to end."

***

Kari was a tiny stick of a girl with straight black hair and dark, luminous eyes. She rarely made eye-contact with anyone, though, preferring to stare meekly at the floor. She was the saddest, most at-risk student I'd ever met.

Her previous, third grade teacher had told me of the brutal father whom Kari had seen strangling her mother before he'd abandoned everyone for his secret other family. I worried that I, Kari's first male teacher, would be inappropriate for her; but then decided I could help heal her by showing that a man could be tender and caring.

Even so, I was horrified when Kari finally completed an assignment, a response to a novel she'd supposedly read. She wrote: "jessica was real upset with her mom because tony had always wanted to run but the music was very loud so the clouds came and it rained and everyone laughed at her but dinner was late and...." Couldn't Kari understand what she'd read? Or, was she unable to write? Or both?

I sat down next to her and attempted find out. She wouldn't speak. In fact, Kari remained silent for weeks. I had no access to her abilities, her thoughts, her feelings, her personality. I couldn't teach her anything at all.

I alerted my school's principal. A school study team met a week later. We quickly agreed Kari was in dire need of both testing and counseling. It fell to me to convince her mom of the latter.

After weeks of emails and phone calls, Kari's mom finally agreed to meet with me at her home on Saturday. I summarized my observations and concerns, handed her a list of local counseling resources, and then ignored her dogged diversions. I just kept insisting, "Kari needs counseling," again and again and again like a broken record, until Mom finally acquiesced. She promised to call for an appointment, but did so only after two more weeks of my nagging.

In December, Kari began to meet with a therapist once a week, and to receive an intense battery of tests at school. In January, the therapist diagnosed "Selective Mutism," a manifestation of severe post traumatic stress. We at school identified significant learning and speech disabilities as well, which really weren't surprising given that Kari had spent several years barely speaking.

By February, she was receiving regular school and community interventions. And I started to notice subtle but definite improvement. Kari still wouldn't converse, but did whisper one-word answers to my private questions. Once she even asked me a question of her own. Then, with an in-class response-to-literature essay, Kari wrote an exemplary paragraph containing a strong topic sentence supported by specific examples from the story. She even added a perfectly punctuated quotation from the text. Amazing!

It was an exciting glimpse of Kari's latent gifts. Eventually, Kari began hanging around me during recess, listening intently to my silly conversations with other kids. She became their friend. She smiled. She laughed.

Finally, in the middle of our end-of-year 4th grade picnic, Kari plopped herself down on the grass next to me and said, "I'm bored." She then proceeded to say three consecutive sentences explaining why. I looked at her with a small smile and nodded, trying to hide my amazement and joy. Kari seemed to be, at least for a moment...normal, happy.

Miracles do happen. Every once in a while, I even get to help them along.

✳ ✳ ✳

There are many miracles in a school.

My responsibilities as an educator include gently nudging youngsters along their long path towards maturity. Sometimes, not so gently. A few kids suffer from the Peter Pan Syndrome, wallowing in childish, often spoiled behavior. I become the wall they so desperately need to hit in order to finally grow up.

Timothy, for instance, accepted responsibility for nothing. Whenever I admonished him, even for something minor, he'd alternately blame others, pout, or even burst out crying.

I remained unsympathetic before such tears, sending Tim out to the hall any time he threw one of his tantrums. "You can come back whenever you decide to behave like a 4th grader."

Then, out of the blue, it happened: I'd told Timothy once again to knock off some sort of inane classroom antic, and I paused for his usual, ugly response before banishing him outside again. Instead, he looked at me wide-eyed, then blurted out, "I'm sorry."

My jaw dropped. Timothy and I stared at each other in surprise. The dramatic moment became too much for him, though, and he buried his head on his desk beneath his arms.

"Well done, Timothy!" I called out. A few moments later, when the rest of the class had begun the task at hand, I stopped by Timothy, his head still hidden, and touched him lightly on his shoulder. "I am so proud of you!"

That same week, another student, Tina, also dug down and discovered a maturity neither of us had expected.

Tina lied habitually. She refused to study for quizzes, learn her multiplication tables, or complete homework with anything but a few careless sentences. Exasperated, I began to just draw a garish line through her scribble and toss it dismissively back onto her desk. "What were you thinking? Do it over." And then she'd cry, of course.

When Tina turned in a re-do that was little better than her first draft, I let her have it after school. "Aren't you embarrassed to watch so many other students progress and grow, crafting work they're proud of, while you're learning little because you won't take pride in yourself or your work?" And then, callously, "Your tears won't make it better. Only your hard work will!"

The next morning, barely suppressing more tears, Tina asked to speak with me. "Mr. Ellison, I know why you're upset with me. But when you yell at me, I just shut down. I can't do anything. Please don't yell at me!"

My draw dropped again. My principal had urged me to tone down my intense, sometimes overbearing classroom personality which had served me well with precocious 8th graders, but which could intimidate nine-year olds. And yet, little, immature Tina had found it within herself to challenge me in an adult manner way beyond her years.

I handed Tina a piece of chocolate from my pocket. "That's for standing up for yourself, Tina. I'm very impressed, and I hope you'll continue to do so all your life.

"Tell you what: I'm going to try very hard not to raise my voice again. Will you please try to improve your work?"

Tina nodded, sniffling and wiping away a tear. She did finally turn in a carefully proofread, multiple-paragraph essay. A miracle!

However, her next three assignments abounded again in careless errors. Oh well. Two steps forward, one step back. At least, for an instant, she and I both saw the courageous, responsible young lady who will eventually emerge.

I'd like to believe I have something to do with such students' blossoming, but recognize how life and children are utterly incomprehensible. I know only how grateful I am that kids possess astounding resilience; and that, when they take a tentative step forward, I get to watch.

* * *

Yes, I had a temper, and it did not serve me or my students well.

I just took my job way too seriously. I knew how essential a great education was for my students and, in fact, the nation. A college degree would provide the kids choices, open the doors of their future to opportunity and, ultimately, power. "Nothing will change until we get people like you," I cajoled, "women and people of color, into positions where you can make a difference. What we do here every day really matters!" I could see it. Why couldn't they?

Worse, I'd traveled often through developing countries and met children who would give anything—anything!—to have the opportunity these kids were squandering. It made me so angry when they wouldn't do their homework, wouldn't even try! What was wrong with them? What was wrong with their parents?

Of course, behind much of my rage was my own insecurity, the fear that I wasn't a great teacher, perhaps not even a good one. Surely some other, better educator could motivate my students. Despite all my effort and passion, I worried I was a failure.

Lisa, my principal and friend, knew me too well and tried to help. She stopped by my class at the beginning of the year once, put her hand on my shoulder and said, tenderly but firmly, "Please try to remember: It's not about you. Dave, you need to learn to let go."

Another friend, Robin, finally got through to me. After listening patiently to one of my exasperated tirades, he replied, "Wow! So, you're God!"

"Excuse me?"

"Yes, you, with your infinite knowledge and wisdom, you alone know precisely what each of your students and their parents must do in order to live their lives well. If only everyone would listen to everything you say and believe, behave exactly as you insist, then all would be well...and you would finally be happy."

After my long, stunned silence, he added, "Dave, your students and their parents are not there to serve you. You serve them. You cannot control them, only yourself. Keep striving, learn from your errors, be satisfied, not with the outcome, but with your best. Let go of the rest. You'll be a lot happier, enjoy your job a lot more...and I suspect your students will enjoy theirs more, too. They might even do a little more homework."

I wished I'd understood that long, long before.

* * *

I exacted my vengeance on my principal, Lisa, for knowing me too damn well. And my students were eager to join me in the fun.

Once when Lisa came in to observe me, in the middle of the lesson I suddenly chastised a student: "Hey, wait a minute, Silvia. You can't participate in this activity. You didn't do your homework last night."

Lisa looked up from her notes in horror.

"Well, Dave," Sylvia replied, repeating the words I'd practiced over and over with her, "you need to learn to let go."

Lisa burst out laughing. After that, she knew we'd have something in store for her every visit.

Another time, I similarly interrupted a lesson to reprimand yet another kid: "Tony, if I remember correctly, you didn't do your homework last night, did you?"

"No Sir," he replied with downcast eyes.

"Well, you know the procedure."

He sullenly got up from his desk, sat on a stool in the front of the class next to the white board, and picked up a large sign I'd hidden folded on the table next to him. He opened it up to reveal printed in bold, red letters, "LOSER!"

That time, Lisa just put her head in her hands and sighed in exasperation, "Mr. Ellison, what next?" She should've known better than to ask.

My favorite hoax took the longest preparation, and involved a lot of practice with the entire class. The principal arrived, sat at my desk and began taking notes, but looking warily around at the class and me. I turned to the students and pointedly gave them their cue: "My children, I am very pleased with you this morning."

All thirty-three of them placed their hands together at their fingertips, bowed their heads down to their desks slowly, and intoned in pious unison, "Thank you, Oh Wise One!"

"You've got to be kidding me!" Lisa cried out.

I just looked back at her with surprised eyes, outstretched arms and replied with melodramatic innocence, "What? What?"

My middle name is Incorrigible...

* * *

The children sang, but I seethed.

At my grade school's final assembly of the year, the choir performed three wonderful songs, "I Believe in Music," "My America," and "Bright Happy Day," often with intricate counterpoint and harmony. Amazing! The loveliness of the music, expressing so eloquently the beauty of the children singing it—American kids of myriad races, creeds and backgrounds, so full of naïve joy and hope—was enough to bring anyone with a warm heart to tears.

Yes, tears of immense gratitude; but also tears of blind rage. As those priceless children, jewels all, sang their own warm hearts out, so many adults in this nation were at that very moment conspiring against them.

Take U.S. Secretary of Education Arne Duncan, for instance. At his request (Oh, the irony!), the National Center on Education and the Economy (NCEE) had reviewed the best educational programs in the world. Its damning conclusion: Duncan's blueprint for education reform had been, at best, a monumental waste of precious time and money. While Duncan had been touting short-sighted quick fixes such as high-stakes standardized testing, merit pay, vouchers and charter schools—guided in defiance of all research by a business/competition/privatization ideology—nations such as Finland, whose schools consistently rank among the best in the world, had implemented much more commonsensical, forward-thinking, even revolutionary strategies.

Most importantly, leading nations had recognized how an educational system can never be any better than its teachers, and so had transformed their teaching professions into one of the most competitive and prestigious. (Finland recruits its teachers from the top 10th percentile of college graduates, The United States from the bottom 30th.) Then, Finland and others had distributed their teachers and funding equitably to all schools and communities.

They'd eschewed once-a-year fill-in-the-bubble testing in favor of broader (including science, social studies and the arts), less frequent evaluation focusing on in-depth knowledge and the ability to apply it creatively. And they'd discarded an archaic age-grouped assembly-line approach to education.

True to form, however, Duncan merely gave lip service to the NCEE report, then called for Congress to reauthorize a revised version of No Child Left Behind. In other words, he chose more of the same, but with some tweaks. He thus doomed The United States to fall even more swiftly from its already precarious eminence.

Arne Duncan betrayed the kids in that choir—again.

Oh, but he was hardly alone. Banks continued to foreclose on their parents, corporations to send their future jobs overseas, and the hidden oligarchy of the nation's giga-rich to diminish their hope for a middle-class life.

Meanwhile, Republicans nationwide, clinging so tenaciously to their no-taxes-except-for-war/lower-taxes-for-the-rich ideology, were at that moment arguing for the evisceration of unions and environmental protections.

Will my school even have a choir next year? Will more than just a few of the youthful singers be able to afford college? Or a home, for that matter? What kind of contaminated world will they inherit? Will there be any Social Security or Medicare when they retire? (If they can retire.)

For the first time in this nation's history, the kids in the choir could expect to live fewer years and at a lower standard of living than their parents. (Read that again.)

I wish all the powerful in this nation—who, because of their unbridled greed, thoughtless ideology or inexcusable cowardice, were betraying the next generation of Americans—had been required to stand by me that morning as my school's choir sang. But, no, like the pilots of the B-52 bombers during the Vietnam War, they didn't have to look into their victims' innocent eyes.

Sing children, I thought. Sing of your oh-so fleeting "Bright Happy Day," and of the "My America" which long ago ceased to be anything more than a legend. Yes, sing—while you still can.

NO CHILD LEFT BEHIND

Turning Education on its Head

The Federal No Child Left Behind (NCLB) Act brought out the worst in teachers and public education. My district and I, unfortunately, were no exception.

When I first read of NCLB and its absurd goal of perfection (100% of American's children proficient), I naïvely believed that my district, hailed by the state superintendent as a model, would wisely choose just to ignore it and to continue the progressive policies and pioneering strategies that had made us great.

All bets were off, however, when our long-standing, visionary superintendent Guy Emanuele retired, to be replaced by the first and worst of successors who systematically dismantled everything. To my horror, nearly everyone went along.

First, in an effort to align ourselves with the new (and inferior to ours) state standards, we abandoned our preeminent performance-based reading and writing assessment programs.

Next, insisting that all our decisions be "data-driven" (and, in the era of NCLB, the only data acceptable was a standardized test score), we adopted the Northwest Education Association testing regime, subjecting our students—even kindergarteners!—to three full batteries of computer standardized tests a year, in addition to the state mandated fill-in-the-bubble one. My district began to worship test scores.

This became apparent one September staff meeting when department leaders shared their analysis of the previous spring's state test. They highlighted the areas where our students had scored the lowest, then zeroed in on the one that had the highest number of questions on the test. Thus, if we focused our teaching on that one skill, we'd get a quick and easy bump in our test scores.

I suggested what seemed obvious (to me), namely that we choose our target skill based upon which one our students most needed to master in order to succeed in their future studies and in life.

The ensuing silence and the many rolling eyes were my first inkling that it was no longer about the kids—which as I came to understand, was the real and insidious effect of No Child Left Behind. Individual student success no longer mattered. Only a school's score did. NCLB had turned education on its head. Kids had become the means to our own end: making ourselves look good (or, at least not so bad) with higher test scores.

For instance, the district eventually banned most field trips, limiting them to one per year per grade, citing how important it was to "keep the kids in their seats."

Important? For the kids, or for the test? I protested, claiming that the best thing we did for children was to get them out of those seats, into the world where they'd garner experiences they'd always remember, and which would help them make sense of their classroom lessons—to no avail.

Later, my principal outlined what a "balanced day" should look like in the classroom, with the recommended class time in minutes for each subject matter spelled out. History appeared at the bottom, in parentheses, to be taught when we could "find the time." Art didn't appear at all. It was logical, really: history and art weren't on the test.

The following year we focused our after-school intervention classes, not on the students who were farthest behind and, consequently, most in need of additional tutoring. No, those unfortunates came to be seen as a sink-hole of time and funds. It would be far more expedient to help the kids just below proficiency since, if they improved their performance just a little, they'd give us another dramatic boost in test scores. (Can you imagine Guy Imanuele permitting such a practice?)

Such cunning strategies soon became standard practice throughout this nation. Another clever ploy was to do nothing to discourage, if not outright encourage drop-outs. Drop-out statistics were notoriously bogus, so there were no repercussions; and the loss of such low-performing students would only increase test scores. In the world of high-stakes testing, there were many, more subtle ways to cheat than to simply change student answers.

Everyone in education knew that No Child Left Behind was wrong, that our methods to protect ourselves from it lacked integrity, and that sooner or later all schools would fail and thereby expose NCLB's absurdity. But, rather than courageously declare how the emperor NCLB had no clothes, we cravenly competed against each other not to be among the first to be labeled a NCLB failure.

Newly elected President Obama offered a brief glimmer of hope, especially given his pledge to base policy on data instead of ideology. However, his choice for Secretary of Education, Arne Duncan, only pursued market-based education reforms including NCLB with even greater vengeance.

My school had succeeded in forestalling the inevitable for a while. In fact, we'd even won the prestigious California Most Distinguished School distinction.

Nonetheless, one of our subgroups finally failed to meet its mandated yearly goal: and, as became the case with the vast majority of Title 1 schools (those receiving federal funds for serving the poorest students), we, too, faced the stigma and sanctions of Program Improvement.

I felt the pressure. I didn't want to let my school down. And so I stooped to "teaching to the test," frantically attempting to "drill and kill" all the math standards prior to the California standardized test.

At the end of the year, I came upon some math projects a colleague had enabled her students to complete dealing with perimeter and area. While my students had dutifully completed the textbook questions on the topic, hers had measured their own bedrooms; then designed on graph paper entire houses, carefully measuring each room's area and perimeter, even calculating how much it would cost to carpet or tile it. My colleague had insisted on teaching a few things well. I had resorted to "covering" everything. Her kids had had a ball, and really learned the topic. Mine had had a bore, but posted higher test scores. I felt ashamed.

My inglorious efforts were in vain. The school remained in Program Improvement, and so faced the next level of sanctions: we had to send a letter to every family inviting them to transfer their children to one of the other two middle schools in the district. We weren't allowed to mention that those schools hadn't met their goals either; or that our test scores were improving faster than theirs; or that similar school comparisons ranked our school much higher than theirs. Since we were the lone Title 1 middle school in the district, we alone faced the sanctions. (Yep. NCLB punished only the poor schools and children.)

Which families chose to transfer? Why, those with kids posting the highest test scores, of course, thus making it even more difficult for us to meet standards. We were doomed.

In more ways than I'd imagined. The district, citing a budget crisis and declining enrollment, decided to close one of its three middle schools. Since only two, including mine, had recently been refurbished and were capable of accepting the influx of hundreds of students from the closed school, you'd think the choice would be easy. It was. The district closed my school since it had fallen under the dreaded Program Improvement. The cost of upgrading the other middle school? More than $20 million. (And, in a bizarre twist, the district sent half the district's middle school kids to my school for a year while upgrading that other one, but renamed mine during the interim the "temporary home" of the other, all to get out from beneath Program Improvement.)

Thus, just as I had betrayed my core values, my district had as well. It destroyed the school that had catered to its poor kids, and insisted that they bus themselves at their own expense to one of the other schools.

This is how No Child Left Behind affected me, my once beloved school, and my previously renowned district. This was reform?

I couldn't accept the tragedy, especially the loss of the school where I'd made my home for eighteen years as mentor teacher and assistant principal. I took a two-year leave of absence from education.

JAMES LOGAN HIGH SCHOOL

Union City, California

The revelation came as a slap in the face.

I'd been teaching my high school unit on WW II and the Holocaust when it hit me: I would have been a Nazi. Yes, I, a passionate long-time progressive activist and educator, would have been a goose-stepping, fascist monster.

When I was a kid, I was a devout Catholic. I believed all the nuns' drivel about how, if I didn't do exactly what they prescribed, I'd surely go to Hell; about how fortunate I was to have been born in the United States, God's bastion of goodness on Earth; about how, if I fought in any war defending America, especially against those awful communists, I'd become a martyr and go straight to Heaven — a place I knew was denied to all non-Catholics, in particular those infidels, the Muslims.

I became an avid Boy Scout, too, doing "my best to do my duty to God and my country, to obey the Scout Law…to keep myself physically strong, mentally awake and morally straight." I loved the flags, the salutes, and especially my scout uniform, with all its badges and rank.

The truth is, I considered myself superior to most everyone else on Earth.

So, oh yes, if I'd been born in Nazi Germany, I would have been first in line to join Hitler's youth corps. And who knows what sort of abominations I might have gone on to do?

What saved me was the opportunity I had after college to live in Spain, to immerse myself in a foreign culture and language—an experience which both opened my eyes to a much wider world, and which forced me to finally accept humility. I learned that no person, faith, country, or race has a monopoly on goodness or evil, or the truth. Indeed, even the great United States is but one economic downturn away from fascism — closer now, perhaps, than ever before.

Today, despite my horror of Hitler, I can view with some compassion the Nazis of the last century and even those who perpetrate atrocities today, such as ICE agents who tear young, helpless refugee children from their parents' arms and lock them into cages. After all, I could easily have ended up just like those goons. There but for the grace of God (or fate or just plain dumb luck) would have gone I.

Don't get me wrong: I'm grateful for much of my Catholic education and my adventures as a boy scout.

Nonetheless, I recognize that education truly is a powerful double-edged sword, one that can be used to brainwash or to challenge, to oppress or to liberate, to ennoble or to deprave.

Our only hope, it seems to me, aside from sending our kids abroad for a year, is to teach children to question all dogmas and authorities; and, above all, to cherish the inherent goodness in themselves and everyone else, no matter who they are, what they look like, what they believe, or where they're from.

This is the only vaccine against becoming a Nazi.

Ellison

PART THREE: RAMBLING ABOUT THE WORLD

"My heart is warm with the friends I make,
and better friends I'll not be knowing.
Yet there isn't a train I wouldn't take
no matter where it's going."

EDNA ST. VINCENT MILLAY

SPAIN

I learned about real fear—mind-numbing, cold-sweating, overwhelming fear—in Spain.

One weekend, my friends took me rock-climbing in the Peaks of Europe, a lovely chain of mountains paralleling Spain's northern coast. On the second pitch of a five-pitch climb (we had to reset our rope five times in order to summit), I'd been trying to get past an extremely difficult section of rock. I'd already fallen several times, saved only by my partner, Gerardo, belaying from above.

After the last fall, however, he'd played out too much slack; and so, when I'd slipped once more, the rope became tangled around my leg. There I was, swinging back and forth against the wall of granite, face down. Desperate, I committed a mortal sin in the world of climbers: I grabbed on to the belaying rope and, hand over hand, heaved myself up past the impassable (for me) passage.

Once I made it safely to the "*reunión*," Gerardo couldn't contain his disgust. "There's only one way to redeem yourself," he explained. "You're leading the next pitch."

I shook my head.

He nodded his and added, *"¡Vete!"* (Go!)

I climbed hesitantly up from the *reunión*, placing too many "*empotradores*" (rubber wedges with small chorded loops) into cracks every few feet, hoping against hope that at least one of them would hold. Somehow I made it, white-faced, to the next *reunión*.

Now it was my turn to belay. "Tell me again how to tie the belaying knot," I called down anxiously to Gerardo.

He did his best. But, when he later joined me on the narrow ledge and saw my poor excuse for a knot, his face became as white as mine. "Well, it's a good thing I didn't fall."

I followed him on the next pitch. At one point, when I clung to a small, one-centimeter ledge by my finger-tips, I looked with horror as the rope led across an immense, smooth rock face to the next *empotrador*. How had Gerardo gotten across? How would I? When I fell, I'd plummet fifteen feet or so, banging myself senseless on the rock in spite of my helmet—if the *empotrador* held.

I tarried for nearly ten minutes, unable to move, Gerardo cajoling me then ridiculing me the whole while.

Finally, with no other choice, I scrambled out onto the rock face. I must have blacked out because the next thing I knew I was on the other side, clinging to a new crack, panting in terror. "Please, God," I pleaded, "get me off this face. I swear I'll never climb again. Just get me down!"

True to that pledge, I have never rock-climbed since.

The problem was that Gerardo and my other Spanish mountaineering friends, eager to include me in their rock-climbing adventures, had taken me bouldering (practicing small climbs) only once, and then flippantly declared me fit to climb mountains. I wasn't. I was way over my head, a danger to myself and others. And so I learned very quickly to hate climbing.

What's my point? How many students have we taught to hate math because a small, elitist committee in Sacramento decreed that all of them, regardless of their maturity or preparation, must take Algebra in 8th grade? These hapless kids probably aren't as afraid as I was. Yet, many have learned to doubt themselves and their abilities just as I did. Perhaps they even pray, "God, please get me out of this math class, and I swear I'll never take one again!"

It was an awful shame for me then, just as it is for them now.

* * *

Spain's new liberal government recently removed monuments to the Spanish dictator, Francisco Franco. The decision placated the many victims and decriers of Franco's four-decade, ruthless, fascist repression, including my Spanish friends.

I recall when one such statue came down back then during renovation of the plaza in Santander. Manolo and Paisa vowed to me that, should it be replaced, they'd blow it up.

The current toppling of Franco's statues caused me to behold with renewed interest some of the monuments in San Francisco.

On the corner of Dolores and Market, there's an impressive statue honoring the city's volunteers who served in the Spanish American War.

A Greek-faced woman gallops a winged horse into battle, cradling a flag in one arm, and brandishing a sword with the other. Beneath her one brave solder falls wounded, another stands stolidly before the enemy, pistol in hand. "First to the front," reads the inscription.

The statue infuriates me. It glorifies war in general, and the Spanish-American one in particular; when, perhaps, I would have been decorated for killing the likes of Manolo and Paisa (or they me). It neglects to mention that the war began under dubious pretexts, and served only to create an American empire.

In the Mission District's Dolores Park stands, appropriately, a giant statue of Miguel Hidalgo, Father of the Mexican War for Independence. A colorful figure if ever there was one, Hidalgo was a priest who gambled, drank, cavorted with women.... He ran afoul of the Catholic hierarchy, not for such sins, but for the unpardonable one of speaking out on behalf of the downtrodden Mexican Natives. Miguel Hidalgo began the revolution on their behalf.

What the monument doesn't reveal, of course, is that the idealistic fellow lost his head for his compassion, literally. And, when it was all over, the only thing changed was that a Mexican oligarchy had replaced the Spanish one, and it exploited the Natives even worse. Hidalgo's is actually a monument to lost, noble causes.

In Yerba Buena Park there's my favorite monument, one I hope doesn't commemorate a lost cause, the Martin Luther King Memorial. There's no statue. Just a wide, beautiful waterfall, behind which extends a walkway and a succession of poignant MLK quotations, culminating with, "No, no, we are not satisfied, and we will not be satisfied until justice rolls down like water, and righteousness like a mighty stream," underscored by the deafening, majestic crash of the brilliantly illuminated cataract.

King's monument is the most honest, and therefore the most powerful. It honors, not just the man, but above all his vision; not what was a while ago, but what might be one day. It captivates, educates, challenges, and inspires. I pray no government ever tears it down.

With this in mind, I know what Spain could do with all those now-defunct Franco Statues. Send them to us here in the United States. Let us erect them throughout our nation, in every park and square—stark reminders of what could happen should we cease to cherish our sacred liberties, our various differences, and our longing for peace.

TIJUANA

Mexico

I never would have volunteered on my own. There were plenty of other seemingly more attractive things to do with my summer vacation. Fortunately, a teacher-friend of mine twisted my arm so hard that, bewildered, I soon found myself among twelve other reluctant volunteers in the slums of Tijuana. We cursed our friends and our fate, but then got to work.

We helped out at an orphanage in a hillside barrio. Two orphans were, for me, especially endearing. The first, a small boy of about seven named José, greeted me every day with a fierce bear hug. He was so starved for affection he wouldn't let go. He didn't want to share me with the rest of the kids. When I finally managed to pry him off, he'd alternately scream in anger or cry in anguish. After a few minutes, he'd sullenly join in the games. He never seemed to really enjoy them, though. José so desperately wanted someone to pay attention to him, to love him, and him alone.

Isabel was no different. Only a year old, she sat stoically in her high chair each lunchtime as I fed her and ten other infants in assembly-line fashion. I'd go down the line, Gerbers in hand, doling out spoonfuls of green glop. "Yum, yum," I lied.

Isabel became my favorite perhaps because of the astounding mess she could make in her diaper. None of the other volunteers wanted to change her, and, well, I was a sucker for her puppy-dog eyes. "Honestly, Isabel," I'd scold, "where did you get it all?" Afterward, I paced the nursery with Isabel's head lying gently on my shoulder. I sang and rocked and tried everything I could to put her to sleep. But as soon as I placed her down, she'd turn her dark, despairing eyes on me and wail, her arms stretching out through the bars of her crib. Nonetheless, I had to go, even though I knew no one would pick her up again until dinner.

As the month all too-quickly drew to a close, I began to wonder if I was really helping any of the orphans. I'd endeared myself to them. Then, like everyone else they'd ever known, I'd soon abandon them and return home, leaving them more forlorn than ever. Perhaps it would have been better if I had never come.

Now, many years later, I realize my short volunteer service was not really supposed to help José or Isabel, but to educate me, to upend my view of the world, and of myself. It did. Ever since, I have never once forgotten my own good fortune, or my responsibility to share it with others.

✳ ✳ ✳

What a fool I was!

After assisting at the orphanage in the mornings, my volunteer friends and I often spent time with other kids at the Tijuana garbage dump.

One afternoon, we donned ridiculous clothes, painted our faces an assortment of silly colors, then headed gleefully out to the dump. We'd hoped to brighten up the lives of the desperately poor children who lived and worked among the refuse by painting their faces, too—visages usually blotched by soot and snot, the result of the eternally smoldering fires.

At the last minute, I'd grabbed three oranges, planning to juggle them and so add to the circus atmosphere. Once there, I initially thought I'd mesmerized the kids with my dexterity. When one of the older children timidly asked for the oranges, however, and, after sharing slices around, she ravenously devoured hers, I understood my folly.

I still had much to learn.

Several days later we decided to take the kids on an excursion to the beach. They gathered anxiously around our van, and I greeted them with a bright-eyed, "Run and get your swim suits, everyone!" They just stared back at me dully. They were wearing the only clothes they owned.

While bouncing our way down to the coast later, quite a few of the children vomited. They all had worms and other parasites.

The irony was that, on that afternoon when I finally accepted the depth of the children's poverty, I also recognized their treasure. Once on the sand, the kids shrieked and splashed with wanton abandon. And, even more remarkably, they took tender care of each other. Teens watched out for the youngsters. Everyone shared the pails and shovels. No one bickered or whined. Those kids had virtually nothing on Earth—nothing except their families and each other. And so, they still found joy.

We volunteers would never have dared take the orphanage kids to the beach. The boys and girls there had everything the garbage dump children lacked—everything except someone who loved them. Worse, most knew their parents hadn't died, but had abandoned them. We tried to teach the orphans to play, but spent most our time breaking up fights, wiping tears. They had clean clothes, full bellies, but remained oh so sad!

I remembered them recently after a failing student had swaggered into class sporting a swanky new warm-up suit, a pair of designer athletic shoes, and the latest, flagship smart phone. I turned away angrily and fumed, "What has he done to earn such rewards? How will he ever learn that one must work hard in life? What were his parents thinking?"

Later, I wondered if those parents, overwhelmed with work or whatever, too often had neglected their son, leaving him to raise himself. Then, in a fit of guilt, they'd showered him with expensive presents, hoping.... But he still wasn't happy, just as the Tijuana orphans weren't.

Even after all these years, I still muse about which of the children I met in Tijuana (and in my classes since) were the most unfortunate, the garbage dump kids or the orphans; and on the shameful tragedy that any child anywhere should face either sort of deprivation.

BOCA LACANTUN

Mexico

"*Menos mal*," said the bus driver. "Less bad that it's the rainy season and the road is wet. A few weeks ago you could hardly breathe for the dust."

Thank God for small blessings, I thought, gripping my seat as we rattled and splashed over miles of chuckholes in the Mexican jungle. We were part of a convoy weaving its way toward the Guatemalan border where hundreds of refugees awaited us, some of the 45,000 refugees who would journey north to Campeche over the next few months.

The exodus from Guatemala had begun in 1981. No one had anticipated the immense numbers, but no one was then aware of the atrocities, the annihilation of Native American pueblos that one priest had described as "nothing less than genocide." Guatemalan refugees were flooding into the dense and uninhabited Mexican jungle.

The Mexican government, unable to stop the migration, feared Guatemala would use the situation to seize Mexican land. The Guatemala government, unable to pursue rebels across the border, believed the refugee camps provided a base to plan future attacks. When Guatemalan soldiers finally started shooting into some camps, Mexico began transporting the Guatemalans north.

Mexican soldiers scoured the mountain jungles for refugees whom they encouraged to come into the camps to be fed, doctored and relocated. Many did not come willingly. Some were tired of fleeing and reluctant to abandon the jungles which so closely resembled home. Others feared anyone in uniform. Rumor had it that force was being used against uncooperative refugees, and that some Mexican soldiers were now firing on them, too. The rumors, true or not, made me uneasy.

The camps deepest in the jungles were near rivers. Refugees could then be floated downstream to Boca Lacantún, my destination, and bussed north. Boca Lacantún was merely a refugee way station.

What happened to the refugees after that was more uncertain. The Mexican economy was in shambles; many said revolution was inevitable. "We can't help but feel sorry for these people," the driver told me. "They are suffering, homeless and hungry. But we are helping our neighbor while letting our Mexican brothers starve."

We arrived at Boca Lacantún early the next morning. Three large thatched pavilions offered temporary shelter to the refugees passing through. Down the road were support facilities made of bamboo and palm leaves: a small hospital, the immigration center and living quarters for the doctors, soldiers and staff. Peasant huts dotted the compound, evidence that this had once been a small, quiet, jungle village.

Soldiers carrying automatic rifles wandered everywhere. Frightened, I went straight to the immigration center to ask permission to volunteer in the camp.

The center was little more than a thatched roof with a wall to one side, and it was crowded with young men in jeans and tee shirts.

The man in charge (Jorge, I was to learn), unshaven and sweating profusely, glanced at my passport, then at me, incredulous. "Fuck!"

He called to another man and ordered, "Run out the pilot (there was a Cessna warming up out on the road which doubled as an airstrip) and ask him if he can get this idiot out!"

The fellow quickly returned, huffing, "He's already overloaded. No way."

"Fuck," Edgar muttered again. Then, he looked back at me, shaking his head. "You've illegally entered a restricted zone. You're under arrest."

This wasn't what I had expected.

I was stripped and searched and interrogated for three hours. Apparently, I was the first American to "infiltrate camp security." Some said I was a CIA spy.

I replied meekly that I'd only begged for a ride on a bus. But here I was, huddled in a corner, trying to ignore the constant, inquisitive glances of everyone who passed through the hut. I sat next to the radio transceiver (so I guess they'd decided I wasn't a spy after all), which blared throughout the day. Since reception was bad and each message had to be repeated slowly, I had no trouble understanding.

A large group of refugees would soon float downriver toward Boca Lacantún. The boats, or *launchas*, would arrive tomorrow afternoon. I waited, watched and listened into the night.

Early in the morning, loud, crackling static awakened me. It woke up others as well who, one by one, emerged sullenly from behind mosquito netting.

One wearing a uniform I mistook for someone in authority. His early morning routine was devoted to brushing, polishing and combing this or that, monopolizing the small mirror that dangled on a bamboo post. He was Alberto.

Francisco, on the other hand, wore only his underwear. With an unkempt beard and a long black pigtail, he brushed past me and swore about the coffee not being made.

These were the camp doctors. They spent the morning taking turns in the hammock suspended in the corner opposite mine.

Four immigration officials occupied the hut as well, but their only chore was to record the comings and goings of the workers and peasants.

A chicken wandered around, then left droppings by a bed. Loud squawking ensued as she was hunted down. The daily rainstorm followed. Several men in underwear lined up beneath a broken gutter pipe—the camp's only shower. A truck spun its wheels in the mud, but no one offered help. The frustrated driver's struggles proved the only entertainment in a long and muggy morning.

Later Alberto and Francisco began a game of dominoes and asked if I'd like to play. In time, I asked Alberto what he did in the camp.

"Nothing," he shrugged. "The first refugees were in a sorry state, but now many doctors are in the camps and on the *launchas*. The serious cases have been weeded out by the time they get here. All I did was dispense aspirin, then turned it over to my assistants. I am a surgeon, damn it."

"They told me I'd be here a week," Francisco complained, "but I've already wasted three."

I asked about the refugees, and Alberto said disgustedly, "You really think they have been so abused? Oh sure, probably in the beginning a few fled in fear. But then everybody jumped on the bandwagon. The land is richer here in Mexico."

Francisco disagreed. He recounted the tales of horror his patients had shared.

I recalled Julio, the 15-year-old Guatemalan I had befriended in Texas six months before. Soldiers had murdered his parents, and he'd fled. I could still see him, his hands thrust deep into his pockets, his dark eyes staring at the ground. *"Muy mala gente"* was all he said. "Some very bad people." It was because of him that I'd wanted to volunteer in a Guatemalan refugee camp like Boca Lacantún.

Food came and I declined. "Eat while you can," I was told. "You never know when you will eat again." Others agreed, complaining about the supply officer who pocketed most of the food budget. "The other day," added another, "they said I could eat refugee food, as if I would eat what they eat." I took a plate and noted the chicken had paid dearly for her crime.

Refugees arrived late in the afternoon. Francisco did not leave his cot; the others did not look up from their comic books. Only Jorge, the senior immigration official, went to get statistics from the boat captains. Otherwise the procession of wretched people passed with little notice.

They trudged in silence through the mud toward the pavilions, all their possessions tied to their backs or balanced on their heads. Many were dressed in the bright, almost fluorescent colors typical of Guatemalan Indians. One young boy wore a Penn State football jersey. Three men struggled beneath a full-sized Amana refrigerator. (What would they have done with that in the middle of the jungle?) Several young mothers suspended infant children beneath their breasts. Their faces showed no emotion except, perhaps, fatigue and the determination to just keep trudging. I got no closer to communicating with them.

Jorge returned and radioed information to headquarters, "Eight *launchas* brought 418 people, 59 families..." He glanced at me doing the mental math and remarked, "That's right. Large, young families that cannot provide for themselves." He resumed his transmission, and watched the refugees filing past.

"It's a terrible situation," I said when he finished.

"Yes," he agreed, "but let's not forget that your country installed the barbaric regime that drove them here."

His words echoed in my head that night as I tossed and turned. Only the incessant sounds from the nearby jungle finally lulled me to sleep.

Jorge spent the next morning glued to the transceiver, trying to resolve a dispute with the boat captains, whose pay had been reduced. The captains balked; no more refugees would be delivered.

A peasant sat down next to me, dejected. He had forgotten his identification papers and had been detained while one of his children went to retrieve them. "When I was a child," he sighed, "they told me all of Mexico was mine. Now I'm not even the *dueño*, the master of my own home." Though he smiled, his frustration was apparent.

When helicopters roared over camp just before noon, Jorge jumped up exclaiming, "The Sub-Secretary! I forgot!" Within seconds everyone had frantically donned their military costumes, stuffed dirty laundry beneath cots, and raised the Mexican flag outside. Jorge admonished me to keep to my chair and stay as inconspicuous as possible.

The Sub-Secretary was on an inspection tour. He walked swiftly toward the river, conversing jovially with his guides. He remained on the bank only long enough to slip and fall in. A pair of replacement pants was quickly found and he changed, then left as abruptly as he had arrived—helicopters disappearing into the sky.

Jorge returned. "I gotta get outa here." He asked if I would like to accompany him and another official to a nearby stream to bathe.

On the way, I wondered why Jorge, a college graduate, kept this position as chief of immigration in a malaria-infested jungle so far from civilization. Perhaps he'd rather be king in Hell than a pauper elsewhere.

He was very aggressive in completing his duties. He went nowhere without his pistol tucked into his belt. Twice I had seen him severely discipline subordinates for seemingly insignificant mistakes. Maybe he thought harshness was necessary in this environment. Alberto thought otherwise. Once, during one of Jorge's tirades, he'd muttered, "If you really want to know someone, give him power."

The bath was refreshing despite the mosquitoes and mud. Jorge basked in the sun afterward, thoroughly contented. I couldn't relax. I was still a prisoner. "How long will you keep me here?"

"I don't know," Jorge said indifferently. "As soon as I finish a few more things...."

"How long will they take?"

"I don't know."

"But you have informed the American embassy of my arrest, haven't you? I have rights."

"You're in Mexico now," Jorge replied "Get used to it."

Busses passed us on our way back to camp, loaded with refugees bound for Palenque. It's ironic, I thought. The refugees would pass by the great Mayan ruins outside Palenque. Many of the refugees still spoke a dialect of the ancient Mayan language. Once the rulers of all Central America, they would return to their palaces as fugitives in a now foreign land.

The next morning agents of the Mexican Federal Police arrived. Everyone tensed as they entered. Jorge shot me a furtive, anxious glance. "*Cállate*," he whispered intently. "Don't say a word."

The *Federales* wore no uniforms, carried automatic rifles, and were loud and abrasive. One brandished an M15 rifle—certainly not government issue—and made it a topic of conversation. "Sylvester Stallone used one of these in *First Blood*," he bragged. "Eh gringo, did you see that movie?" He didn't wait for my reply, but described the movie's graphic portrayals of the M15's power.

As the conversation continued, I figured out what the *Federales* did and why they carried such weapons. They protected the drug trade flourishing in the mountain jungles, and smuggled the drugs north past military checkpoints beneath the refugee busses.

Perhaps, then, it was no surprise that the police became increasingly annoyed with my presence in the hut. They interrogated me repeatedly and pointlessly. They traded jokes extolling the pleasures of raping American women.

One of the immigration agents tried to reassure me during dinner. "Don't worry," he said. "They're just trying to frighten you."

"They're doing a good job."

After dinner the *Federales* taunted me again, threatening to personally guide me to the other camps I had wanted to see—a one-way tour, I feared.

"You don't want to do that," Jorge said in a meager defense. "I sort of like the gringo."

I whispered to him, "They can't take me anywhere, can they? You arrested me so you're responsible for me."

"You think so?"

Terrified, I finally realized the federal agents answered to no one and could do with me whatever they pleased. I thought of the death squads who had "disappeared" so many others into the Central American jungle.

Late that evening Jorge woke me up with a nudge and whispered, "Shhhh! Get up. We're leaving." I didn't have to be told twice.

It was a long trip back to Palenque. Rain pounded the windshield and I became reacquainted with the same chuckholes that had jostled me four days before. Four days? It seemed only yesterday that I'd been chatting with the bus driver.

I thought of him and the others—the doctors, soldiers, peasants and refugees, all the prisoners of Boca Lacantún. And I realized that I was the only one who had really wanted to be there. And I was the only one who would soon be free.

***

The truth is, the ride back to Palenque was harrowing. I feared that the *Federales* had simply ordered Jorge to drive me out into the jungle and shoot me. Indeed, he made me sit in front with the driver while he sat directly behind. I surreptitiously opened up my tiny Swiss Army knife in my pocket, a pathetic but noble attempt to go down with a fight.

It wasn't needed. When we arrived the next morning, Jorge took me straight to the immigration office, called the hotel where the other officials were staying, and told them all to come in right away.

"Is that necessary?" I asked.

"The more people who know of you," Jorge explained, "the harder it is to disappear you."

The others were eager to meet me. They'd never arrested an American before, much less one who spoke Spanish. They took turns trying to type out my arrest paper, pestering me with questions, most of which had nothing to do with the bureaucracy at hand. In the end, since I was the one man there would could type decently, I completed the paperwork myself, telling stupid jokes the whole while.

When I finished, there was a long, uncomfortable silence. Finally, Jorge said, "We're supposed to lock you up now."

I shrugged my shoulders in resignation.

"Nah!" he laughed. Let's go get a beer!" We drank for the rest of the day.

Later, the immigration officials found a bed in one of their hotel rooms for me because they refused to put me into jail. The fellows got me even drunker at a dance club that night, then goaded me into asking a pretty Mexican girl to dance.

"Let me show you how we gringos conquer the ladies!" I bragged.

After a dance, I bought the girl a drink at the bar and attempted to get to know her. "So, what do you do?"

"Nothing," she replied.

"What would you like to do?"

"Marry me a gringo."

I gulped my beer.

Just then, I felt an aggressive tap on my shoulder. I turned around to meet an apparently angry man.

"Who the hell are you?" I asked impatiently. (I was drunk.)

"I'm her uncle! Who the hell are you?"

I quickly apologized, then explained, "Actually, I'm under arrest! See those guys over there? They're my jailers. They dared me to ask your niece to dance." I told him the whole story of my time in Boca Lacantún.

"Wow!" he exclaimed when I was done with my tale. "What did you think of those *Federales*?"

I told him exactly what I felt, using every Spanish expletive I knew.

"Hmmm." He reached into his back pocket for his wallet, opened it up to reveal his *Federales* badge. "I'm second-in-command for the entire region."

My eyes narrowed. "You son of a bitch!" I exclaimed. (Did I mention I was drunk?)

He looked at me dumbfounded, then called out, laughing, "Bartender, get this man another beer!"

At the end of the evening, he invited me to be his niece's companion the following day when he and his wife went for a picnic at a local national park, *Aguas Azules* (Blue Waters). It was a lovely, relaxing date beside a breathtaking waterfall. "If I had known being arrested was going to be so much fun," I remarked, "I would have done it long ago!"

Two days later, though, one of the officials escorted me by bus to Mexico City where I was finally locked up in the federal immigration prison. The party was over.

My mom had always said, "When life gives you lemons, make lemonade!" I'd traveled to meet new people, I mused. Now I was incarcerated with all sorts of people from everywhere, and they had nothing better to do than talk with me. Cool! Since virtually all of them had hoped to cross into the United States (and would likely try again), I figured I might as well teach them English.

I conducted two classes daily. Soon, my prison-wide nickname was "*El Profe* (The Professor). One of my students, Carlos, who'd come from Guatemala (whom the Mexican guards had beaten severely leaving permanent scars), remained my friend for the rest of his life.

But, how long would I be in prison? I was once taken to a processing center downtown where I spent the day in a glass cage surrounded by officials chatting across their desks, reading newspapers, laughing on the phone, but processing no one. I began to worry.

A week later I returned to that cage. This time I shared it with a very attractive, but really upset American woman. "God damn it!" she fumed, even though we weren't supposed to talk. "They arrest me like this every year, just to harass me. I'll be out by the end of the day, but this really pisses me off!"

"Well," I whispered, "when you're out, could you please inform the American Embassy that I'm here? My name is Ellison. David Ellison...."

An embassy attaché interviewed me in prison a few days later; and soon enough (too soon for me since I'd been having so much fun), yet another amiable immigration official (who shared how worried he was because he'd inadvertently left information about his mistress back at home for his wife to find) escorted me to the border town of Matamoros where I was summarily deported. I was not to return for five years.

When I crossed back into a land where *The Bill of Rights* was still respected (unlike now), I dropped to my knees and kissed the ground. I was home.

Now, thirty-five years later, the memory of that wild adventure, when I so blithely wandered among such desperate people and dangerous circumstances, fills me with shame—and wonder. I could, should have died in Mexico. Were I still religious, I'd say I had a particularly attentive guardian angel; although, I suppose that's the role Jorge played in my life.

The irony is that I've returned to Mexico often. In fact, my partner and I recently purchased a retirement home in Ajijic, just south of Guadalajara. I'll teach English there, and volunteer in a local orphanage.

So, I will eventually die in Mexico. And that will be a blessing.

ESTELI

Nicaragua

"*Barricada! Barricada!*" The voice of the paperboy rang out crisply amid the din of the Esetlí town plaza in northern Nicaragua. Flanked by the town hall, the church, a hotel and a theater, the plaza bustled with activity from sunrise to sunset. Old women with no teeth sold fruit and vegetables, young boys with no shoes shined those of others, and a gringo sat writing letters to his friends. It was hard to believe that Estelí lay in a war zone, just 25 miles from the Honduran border.

The paperboy followed his usual route past the statue in the center of the plaza and along the benches arranged neatly beneath the surrounding palm trees. This afternoon he wore the same tattered shirt as always, which was clumsily tucked into the pants he had out-grown years ago. When he caught sight of me, one of his regular customers, his face lit up in a smile. His name was Remigio, and he was 12 years old.

Remigio made change quickly, drawing out an impressive wad of bills—all utterly valueless because of rampant inflation. Business attracted business, and before Remigio could complete the transaction, another young vendor appeared at my elbow who presented me with a large carton of gum boxes.

"Chiclets, David?" (He pronounced my name with a thick, Spanish "Da-beeth.")

"No, not today, Manuel."

Instead of dashing off in search of more sales, though, Remigio and the smaller Manuel plopped themselves down beside me on the bench. Perhaps they were less shy now that they were together. They sat in silence, their eyes dancing from my baseball cap and red beard to my muddied tennis shoes. Gringos sure dress funny.

I broke the ice when I asked Remigio about school. He said he was in the sixth grade. Manuel, a second-grader, was incredulous. He grabbed a newspaper and demanded Remigio read it. When Remigio did so easily, Manuel looked at me inquiringly and I nodded my head. We were both impressed.

But how did they manage to learn so much while wandering the streets all day?

Manuel explained that both he and Remigio attended morning classes, and worked only in the afternoons. Ah, they must be glad to be on summer vacation and have their mornings free. No, no...now they spent the whole day plying their wares on the streets. Besides, they liked school. "One must better oneself," Remigio explained soberly. "We must continue forward," and by "we" he meant more than just Manuel and himself.

"Children aren't so enthusiastic about school in the U.S.," I said. I opened my notepad to a new page and began to draw a map of The States.

The kids leaned over, intensely curious. Remigio asked, as if blind to the crudeness of my sketch, "Can you draw?"

I paused and looked at him. In an instant I understood why the boys had stopped to chat with me, and I was embarrassed that it had taken me so long. In Nicaragua, ever since the Sandinistas had begun to build schools, children begged, not for money, but for pencils; and here I sat with a mechanical one, probably the first one the boys had ever seen.

"No. Can you?" I responded, proffering Remigio my pencil and note pad. He seized them both eagerly and immediately set to work. His brow furrowed. He held his breath during each pencil stroke. But he made no mistakes, no erasures. He'd hesitated only long enough to figure out how to advance the lead.

Remigio could really draw well. With careful patience, he traced the lines of a man's face—first the eyes, then the glasses, then a small beard and moustache—and suddenly I gasped silently. Remigio was drawing Carlos Fonseca.

Fonseca had been the founder of the F.S.L.N. (Sandinista National Liberation Front) which had led the revolution against the hated American-sponsored dictator, Somoza. He'd also been a Marxist, and had received much of his revolutionary training in the Soviet Union and

Cuba. After his death, the Sandinistas had joined forces with other opposition groups, and had become more moderate. Now in power, however, the Sandinistas appeared to resurrect Fonseca's ideology. They radically and often forcibly changed the entire fabric of Nicaraguan life. They silenced opposition newspapers. They developed close ties with Cuba and the Soviet Union.

I was frightened by Remigio's drawing. There were many dissidents in Nicaragua who claimed that communist indoctrination was at the root of the Sandinistas' commitment to education; that the Sandinistas edited the textbooks Remigio studied with the same zeal as they did the newspapers he sold. Was Remigio's drawing an example of such indoctrination? By teaching Remigio to idolize Fonseca, were the Sandinistas encouraging him to embrace Marxism as well?

On the other hand, why shouldn't Remigio admire Fonseca? Fonseca's efforts had led to the end of forty years of tyranny, and of an even longer period of American intervention/domination. There was a famous legend abut the time Fonseca had come upon one of his soldiers teaching peasants to fire a rifle. "*Y también enséñales a leer.*" (And also teach them to read.) The Sandinistas had heeded his words and built hundreds of schools and hospitals. They'd vastly reduced illiteracy and virtually eliminated diseases such as Polio and Malaria, earning international acclaim, including a prestigious UNESCO award. Fonseca had fought and died for such a free, educated, and healthy Nicaragua. Perhaps it was only natural that Remigio would honor him as a founding father, much as American kids do Washington.

Still, I didn't know how to react to Remigio's drawing, just as I remained ambivalent about the Sandinistas in general. I was happy to see that, as a final touch, Remigio drew a dove of peace on Fonseca's shoulder. Yet, I thought dryly, it certainly was not peace that Fonseca had given his country.

Remigio finished and looked up expectantly, oblivious to my musings. After a pause, I told him that his drawing was very, very good. And, truly, it was.

Manuel, who had been waiting patiently, now pleaded for a turn with the pencil and paper. But when he had both in his hands, he became suddenly tentative. He didn't know what to draw. Remigio was a tough act to follow. Manuel stalled by advancing the lead and then retracting it again several times, and then finally began his own creation. He drew a house. It had square windows, a rectangular door, and a pointed roof—no different from a house any American second-grader might draw. Manuel leaned back and appraised his work, comparing it to Remigio's. Dissatisfied, he returned to his house and made many strange additions: a wide circle around the base and five dark protrusions with flames coming out. I couldn't make heads or tails of the drawing until Manuel placed a large moon at the top of the page and a tiny Earth at the bottom. He had transformed his house into a space ship.

What Manuel lacked in skill he made up in creativity. His lines were straight and simple, his subject innocent. I wondered how a few more years of Sandinista education would change him. Soon he might be drawing just as well as Remigio, and with just as many political overtones.

By the time Manuel had finished his second drawing, a small crowd of other young boys had gathered around the park bench. Each offered praise and criticism, and each demanded time with the pencil. Before long, seven pages of my note pad were full of cars, tractors, airplanes, boats, and even a large bull, which Remigio had added. No one else could match his talent. And no one else had felt inspired to make any allusions to the Sandinista revolution. In fact, the primary concern of these kids seemed to be to collect discarded cigarette wrappers, valued currency in the subculture of Nicaraguan youth. Perhaps I'd exaggerated the significance of Remigio's portrait of Fonseca.

The kids might have spent the rest of the afternoon drawing had they not been interrupted by loud horns and heavy rumblings. A small convoy of military trucks was passing through Estelí on its way north towards the border—reinforcements in response to a recent Contras attack there. (The United-States-sponsored Contras were former members of Somoza's vicious national guard.)

As usual, the Contras' targets had been new schools, hospitals and agricultural cooperatives like the one where I was volunteering here in Estelí. This time a Contra mine had blown up a civilian bus, killing 34 peasants, most of them women and children. (President Reagan called the Contras "freedom fighters.") It was no surprise that, despite food shortages, press censorship, and a myriad of other complaints against the Sandinistas, Nicaraguans still viewed the Contras as the enemy.

The boys around me quickly dispersed and joined the cheering crowds lining the streets. The young soldiers on the trucks raised their rifles and waved Sandinista flags. Behind their euphoric faces, however, I imagined fear. The soldiers would quickly leave the applause behind and face the long, rugged road north. And they knew there might be more mines awaiting them.

As the rumbling faded in the distance, I glanced over the many drawings in my note pad, returning finally to Remigio's sketch of Fonseca. I studied it a long time. Fonseca's image overwhelmed the innocence of the other drawings. Indeed, should the peace process fail, the Contra War would soon be an integral part of all these kids' lives. The few pencils they were able to get their hands on would be replaced by rifles; and they would find themselves on similar trucks, en route to defend Fonseca's revolution.

A shadow passed over Fonseca's portrait, and I looked up to find Manuel standing over me. "Are you sure you don't want some Chiclets?"

"OK, Manuel, give me a packet." I gave him the money and asked, "Want to draw some more?"

He appeared tempted, but shook his head sheepishly. Without his friends, Manuel was a shy as ever. He silently shouldered his carton and left. His bare feet carried him swiftly away through the busy streets of Estelí.

YAJALON

Mexico

I returned to Mexico. I ended up in a small pueblo in Chiapas, the southernmost state, to spend a month volunteering at a mission for Native children. But I had a week beforehand to wander as a tourist, practice my Spanish, and gorge myself on tacos while trying to avoid Montezuma's Revenge.

Before I did anything else, though, I had to make a solemn pilgrimage back to *Los Niños Héroes* (the Children Heroes). I went to pay homage, and to beg forgiveness—for me and my country.

Their monument stands guard just outside the castle atop Grasshopper Hill, overlooking the beautiful Chapultapec Park in the middle of Mexico City. At its base, a small plaque reads in Spanish, "To the memory of the young cadets who here gave their lives, defending their homeland from the invader."

During my first trip to Mexico ten years before, standing before the monument amid a large crowd of tourists from all over the world, I turned to the man next to me and flippantly asked, "Who were the invaders?"

He looked back at me in astonishment. Others walked away shaking their heads.

Like them, I still wonder how it was possible for me, a United States citizen, a college graduate, and a teacher no less, to be so very ignorant.

I'd heard of the Mexican American War, of course; but I knew nothing more than the fact that the United States had won. I assumed it was merely another example of my country "making the world safe for democracy." The United States certainly had never invaded anyone. (Yes, I was that stupid.)

I'd learned and matured quite a bit during the next decade. So, when I returned to the Children Heroes, it was with a newfound humility. I finally recognized the sacredness of their story, their sacrifice:

In 1846, President Polk was determined to fulfill America's "Manifest Destiny." He vowed to extend our borders all the way to the Pacific. When Mexico refused to sell the Southwest, Polk used a Texas border dispute as a pretext for war. (Even Abraham Lincoln referred to the resulting conflict as a "trumped up war.") American forces invaded on three fronts and marched all the way to Mexico City.

The city's last defense was the castle on top of Grasshopper Hill where there was a military academy. The young cadets fought tenaciously, valiantly, futilely. When it was evident that all was lost, six of them, *Los Niños Héroes*, could not bring themselves to surrender, and fought to the death. According to legend, one wrapped himself in the Mexican flag and leapt off the ramparts to his death.

Los Niños Héroes symbolize so much of Mexico's noble yet tragic history. I suppose it's not a surprise that American textbooks don't mention them; but it is a terrible shame, particularly in light of NAFTA (North American Free Trade Agreement). If we Americans are ever to understand our southern neighbor, we must learn of Mexico's Children Heroes.

I returned to their monument to make a solemn pledge: I would tell their story to all my students, every year. And I have. My students will never be as ignorant as I once was.

✳ ✳ ✳

Thanks to Father Loren, Lucio would probably never join the Zapatistas.

Lucio was a Native Tzeltal from *"Los Altos"* (The Highlands), the isolated mountainous region of Chiapas, in Southern Mexico. His ancestors had sought refuge in these cloud-enshrouded, verdant peaks, fleeing Spanish conquest, slavery and disease.

Four hundred years later, he and his people still led a precarious existence, barely surviving on a meager diet of corn and beans. They had few roads, schools, or hospitals. Electricity and plumbing were rare, while illiteracy and infant-mortality were the highest in Mexico. And every year the lowland ranchers stole even more of their land, while paying even less for the Natives' one cash crop, coffee.

It really was no surprise that some Natives had finally rebelled, especially after NAFTA all but doomed their communal lands, called *ejidos*. Naming themselves after the famous hero of the Mexican Revolution, Emiliano Zapata, a small army of poorly armed Zapatistas had seized four towns in Chiapas six months before my arrival. Their demands had been a litany of basic human rights: "Work, land, a roof over our heads, food, health, education, independence, freedom, democracy, justice and peace."

The Zapatistas had since melted back into the hills, while a huge Mexican army occupied the lowlands. (I'd had to lie my way through the army checkpoints, claiming I was going to visit an old ranch-owner friend. If I'd revealed I was on my way to volunteer at a mission for Native children, I'd have been brusquely turned away.) Although negotiations had broken down, an uneasy peace prevailed. Everyone seemed to be waiting with baited breath for the national elections in August. After that, who knew?

No matter what happened, I was pretty sure Lucio would avoid the violence. Father Loren, an American priest from Los Angeles, had offered him and 50 other Native children an alternative: education.

Supported primarily by donations from the United States, Fr. Loren had built two boarding houses in the small town of Yajalón, one for boys and one for girls. The houses enabled poor kids from many far-flung Native villages to attend the local schools.

It was Fr. Loren who'd invited me to volunteer for a month that summer. (I'd had to agree to leave—either on the next bus, or following a Native into the hills—if anything flared up.)

I couldn't help much in so short a time, but I figured out his devious plan. Every now and then he nonchalantly remarked, his eyes rolling up to the ceiling, "Gosh, I sure wish I could send more of these kids off to college. If only I could find some people to sponsor them." It wasn't a terribly hard sell since I'd been immediately impressed with Father Loren, the boarding houses, and the kids like Lucio who thrived in them.

Not everyone was smiling. An educated Native is a powerful one, who at the very least will no longer submit to exploitation or injustice. Thus, ranchers perceived Father Loren as a threat to their way of life. Some had accused him of inciting the Zapatistas, and even of supplying them with arms. They blamed foreigners like him for the war.

I wished the ranchers could see and accept one very important point: Change must come to Chiapas. The only question is, Will it come peacefully or through civil war?

Father Loren encourages would-be Zapatistas to take up books instead of arms. While I was at the mission, Lucio became the first person from his Tzeltal village to graduate from high school. The next fall, with a promised scholarship from me, he hoped attend the university in Mérida to pursue something so much more powerful and peaceful than a rifle: a college diploma.

(Note: One week after I left the mission in Yajalón, soldiers came in the night and, at the point of a gun, expelled Fr. Loren from Mexico. I was never able to sponsor Lucio.)

✳ ✳ ✳

For a moment I forgot the kids were Native American.

We'd been playing soccer together at the mission boarding house, and, for a while, they seemed no different than my students back in California. As the game wore on, though, one kid began to limp. "Ampollas," the hapless forward explained with a cheerful shrug. (Blisters) His toes peeked out from ragged boots. I looked around and finally noticed with embarrassment that I was the only one on the field with decent shoes or even socks.

Compared to most of my students back home, these Native Americans (Tzeltal and Ch'ol) were desperately poor. There were many other differences. For one, they appeared to be very young. They were smaller than I, even though they were at least 16 years old—probably another manifestation of their poverty, a poor diet growing up. Heck, back in California most kids their age towered over me. Here, I was a giant—a cause of much mirth as I regularly bumped my head on the rafters of the cooking shed.

The Native kids acted younger as well, more innocent. One afternoon, for instance, I came upon a small group of boys giggling nervously, while poking at something on the ground with a stick. It turned out to be a smuggled-in condom. They were afraid to even touch it! I laughed at their naiveté, but couldn't decide whether it was healthy or not.

One thing was for sure: Those kids worked much harder than my California students. They woke up at 5 am so they could hike to school by 7. Since there were few textbooks, they spent most of the day copying endless notes off the board. Nonetheless, by senior year they'd study Calculus.

At 2 pm, they retuned to the mission for dinner—usually corn tortillas and beans. Once a week, they might get some chicken. Afterward, they had two hours of chores, which was how they earned their keep at the mission. They took turns looking after chickens, rabbits, pigs and goats. Others tended the fields of beans, corn, coffee and alfalfa. On Saturdays, they toiled for 7 hours. Only Sundays were free, when they washed their clothes by hand and caught up on their homework. And they did it all without anyone having to nag.

Yet, it was their effervescent joy I remember most, a lightness of heart evident everywhere, from their spontaneous laughter in the chicken coop to their silly songs in the dormitory. Perhaps they were happy because they knew they had been given a grand opportunity. Unlike most of their friends who remained isolated back in their mountain villages, they could attend school. They could aspire to be much more. Or, maybe, because of their humble beginnings, they simply had learned to enjoy simple pleasures, to appreciate life and each other.

I'd come to the mission expecting to feel sorry for the poor Mexican Native children. Instead, in spite of all their hardships and disadvantages, all their blisters, I became convinced that, in many profound ways, they were better off than most of my students back in California.

* * *

I kept telling myself I wasn't a complete idiot. But then I'd screw up again, and the mission kids would chuckle and shake their heads in amused exasperation: "Poor Dave! He really tries, but he'll never make a farmer."

One day, after nearly a month of practice, I felt I had finally learned to milk a goat. The first time I'd tried, I'd tugged and pulled and twisted that dang udder until I thought I'd break it, but no milk came out. Eventually, I'd learned how to squeeze my thumb and index finger together to close off the base of the udder, while using the rest of my fingers to force the milk out in warm, narrow jets into the stainless steel bucket below. It was easy!

Or, so I'd thought. Then Jaime, my adolescent mentor, grew tired of waiting for me to finish, and he'd stepped out to complete the rest of the chores.

That's when Dancha, the brown goat, betrayed me. I didn't understand it. She'd always been friendly, nibbling my shirt every morning in affection. But, she suddenly began to squirm, upsetting my aim so that most of her milk ended up on my pants leg or the ground.

I didn't get angry, though. I gently stroked her side, whispering sweet, soothing nothings, pleading with her to calm down. She responded with a loud, obnoxious bawl and kicked over the bucket. Jamie returned and helped me clean up the mess, grinning the whole time. Afterward he deftly finished milking Dancha who, of course, submitted to him docilely. I hated her!

Working in the cornfield later that afternoon didn't go any better. To begin with, after no more than half an hour, I had a new set of blisters. The kids, wielding their own hoes around me, feigned their usual sympathy. Yet, I knew they wondered how anyone could have such delicate hands. I hoed even more furiously to prove I wasn't a wimp, which only made the blisters worse.

Worst of all, the little plants all seemed the same to me. Several times one of the kids looked over and remarked—with a patient tact that was really beginning to annoy me—"Um, Dave, I'm afraid you just tore out another corn plant. The one you left next to it is a weed."

"I knew that!" I responded irritably, and then stomped off for one more drink of water. The kids, meanwhile, worked on without any sort of rest or refreshment. What were they, camels?

Still, although I felt inept at everything—from sharpening a machete to shoveling pig manure—I did manage to learn something: the importance of humility. A young student, for instance, accepts the fact that he's ignorant, and so eagerly seeks out instruction, expecting to make mistakes. An adult (especially a teacher!) on the other hand, has grown accustomed to competence. I suddenly recognized that I was far more at ease giving advice than receiving it, and so balked when some impertinent snot-nosed know-it-all like Jaime tried to show me the correct way to grasp an udder.

Once I swallowed my pride and let the kids teach me, the old dog Dave was finally able to learn a few new tricks.

✳✳✳

Everything has its price.

Lydia came from a small Native village tucked away in the mountains. There, her parents, grandmother, and four younger brothers shared a one-room dirt-floored, windowless hut, constructed of rough-hewn planks of wood and corrugated aluminum. Acrid smoke from the cooking fire did nothing to discourage the flies.

But Lydia was oblivious to them, as she was to her poverty. She'd never known anything else. In fact, she considered herself fortunate because a narrow dirt road had finally connected her village with the nearest town of Yajalón. Next had come electricity for her home's one garish light bulb, dangling just above the faded picture of Our Lady of Guadalupe. Who could ask for anything more?

Lydia's parents had wanted more, at least for her, and they'd guessed that an education was the best way to get it. So they sent Lydia off to the mission boarding house for girls in Yajalón.

From the moment Lydia set foot in the boarding house, she was awed. First she was shown to her own cot of burlap stretched over a wood frame. Such luxury! There was running water, a shower, a toilet, and even toilet paper! In the kitchen hummed a refrigerator. Just out back purred the washing machine. Why, she'd moved into a palace!

Then her education began. At school she learned to speak Spanish instead of her native language, Zteltal. She quickly mastered the three R's, as well. She was, in fact, very bright, an outstanding student. Her parents were so proud!

They were not aware of all the lessons Lydia was learning, though. She taught herself to twist and shake to Michael Jackson's *Thriller*. And she became addicted to television soap operas, where she learned of "modern" life styles, capitalistic values. Her horizon thus broadened, she aspired to so much more than she ever could have imagined back in her small Native village.

Lydia graduated from high school, and, after the ceremony, she asked me to take a picture of her with her parents. As I focused the camera, I marveled at her miraculous transformation: Dressed in low heels, a sharp blue dress with white trim, a stylish hair-do and lipstick—Lydia was radiant!

Next to her stood her parents, unsmiling. Her mother wore the traditional Tzeltal blouse with the brightly colored border she had woven herself. Her father stood barefoot, clutching his straw hat. Perhaps they were simply bewildered. Or maybe they understood the terrible price they and their daughter had paid.

What price? Next year, Lydia will be off to college far from home. When she finally returns to her parents in their humble house, will she come to stay? Will she wear the traditional dress of her people? Will she join her mother in pounding clothes clean in the creek? Will she want to marry any of the young men she left behind? Indeed, will she still be Tzeltal in anything but name?

Lydia's education has been and will be a wonderful opportunity, a marvelous achievement. But I wonder if, in exchange for it, she will have to give up her family, her village and her culture.

ROME

Italy

I was devastated. I gazed out over the Roman Forum and saw only ruins. Oh, I'd seen many photographs over the years, of course. Somehow I'd still hoped the site would be more impressive in person, evoking the mighty empire Rome had once been, leaving me speechless, awestruck. Instead, I felt only profound disappointment.

I'd first become enthralled with Rome, and all ancient history for that matter, in high school. My Latin teacher, Mr. Knittle, had guided me through a painstaking translation of *Caesar's Gallic Wars: "Gallia est omnis divisa in partes tres."* (All of Gaul is divided into three parts.) It had seemed interminably dry, at first. Then we'd read of Caesar's epic siege of Alesia:

Caesar had pursued his most daunting Gallic enemy, Vercingetorix, to the heavily fortified town of Alesia. He ordered his troops to dig two deep trenches and use the dirt to build two massive walls in concentric circles around Alesia, together extending more than twenty-five miles. The inner trench/wall would trap Vercingetorix, the outer one protect Caesar's forces from Gallic reinforcements.

It was a brilliant feat of engineering, but still a desperate gambit, since the Romans were hopelessly outnumbered. In fact, shortly after the fateful, final battle commenced, the Gallic reinforcements breached the Roman outer walls, and all seemed lost. But, Caesar's luck had not yet run out. Vercingetorix's had.

It had been a fantastic story, and after translating it, I'd vowed I would one day touch a Roman aqueduct, trod a Roman road, visit the Roman Forum....

So, I'd dreamed of this pilgrimage to Rome for nearly three decades. As I beheld the tumbled foundations with nary a pillar left standing, however, I recalled King Ozymandias' ironic boast about his similarly shattered stone visage, "Look upon my works, ye mighty, and despair!"

I sighed and walked on. Nearby stood Constantine's arch of triumph, inundated with tourists who paused only long enough to snap a digital image without actually looking at what they'd just photographed.

Adjacent loomed the Coliseum, with some enterprising young Italians stealing the show in front. Costumed as Roman soldiers with plastic breastplates and swords, they charged a few Euros to take your picture with them. One of them played Caesar while the others, laughing, pretended to stab him. Blasphemy! "It was the senators who assassinated him, you idiots," I muttered to myself, then stormed away.

This was Rome? No, this was but Rome's pathetic grave, now defiled utterly.

And then it hit me. It was as if an angel had spoken just as one had outside Jesus' tomb: "Why seek ye the living among the dead?" (*Luke* 24:5). This wasn't Rome. Rome hadn't perished. No, Rome yet thrived in our literature, our language, our architecture, our government...forming the foundation for so much of what we in the West had built and become.

Rome could be found, not amid its ruins, but within the living pages of so many texts and histories. What is more, it had taken a teacher to lead me to them, and, ultimately, to teach me to revere them. I didn't have to travel to the Forum to discover Rome. In fact, I'd doubt I ever could have found it there. (The other tourists with me certainly hadn't.) I needed only to enter Mr. Knittle's classroom.

It had taken me thirty years to come full circle and finally understand: I'd gone to Italy hoping to appreciate Rome as never before. Instead, I learned to appreciate my teacher, Mr. Knittle, and the power of all teachers to inspire in a way no stone monument ever could.

GHANA

West Africa

Children singing woke me up my first morning in Ghana. I stepped out onto the hotel balcony—bleary-eyed, jet-lagged, but still both ecstatic and curious—to find a junior secondary school just below (grades 7 to 9), its walls painted the same colors as the students' uniforms: brown bottoms with yellow tops. The innocent, joyful music was an encouraging beginning to a six-week study tour of Ghana.

I'd come with 24 other lucky educators who'd been chosen from a pool of nearly 300 applicants to participate in a National Endowment for the Humanities Summer Seminar for Teachers. Our purpose became clear later that same morning when, while visiting a senior secondary school (grades 10 – 12), a student had bitterly asked why Americans had such negative perceptions of Africans.

"Ignorance," I answered. "Most American kids know nothing of Africa. That's why we've come: to listen, to learn, and later to share our discoveries with our students back home."

The Ghanaian schools fascinated us, of course. The Europeans—Portuguese, Dutch, and finally the British, who triumphed—built the first mission schools here in the late 15th Century. In addition to stealing the continent's natural and human resources (gold and slaves), they'd hoped to convert the Africans to Christianity; and, perhaps even more importantly, to train a small native elite just enough to help administrate the empire. (The Europeans had no choice since they kept dying from Malaria.)

Ironically, it was that same elite, led by one Kwame Nkrumah (Ghana's first president), who, in 1957, finally won independence. Such is the power of education: Even when used as a tool of exploitation and oppression, it ultimately empowers and liberates. Not surprisingly,

Nkrumah made free universal education through junior secondary school a national priority.

In Ghana—where people still speak more than 60 indigenous languages, still pray to Jesus, Allah, or myriad traditional deities, and still look first to the village chief for leadership—education serves also as an essential tool for nation-building. Thus, "creating unity while honoring diversity" is not just a slogan for Ghanaians. It's a matter of survival, a way of life.

Primary school instruction begins in the local language; but by junior secondary school, English predominates. (You can usually tell how educated people are by how well they speak English.) The national curriculum contains a heavy dose of religious and moral education, but includes and honors Christianity, Islam, and traditional religions equally. Ghanaian schools follow the British model. In most classes students merely copy endless paragraphs off the board into their notebooks. Corporal punishment is customary, expected.

For most students, dropping out is not an embarrassment, but an inevitability since, after junior secondary school, proficiency tests and mounting fees weed kids out, the latter proving the most daunting obstacle. (Wherever I went in Ghana, teens begged me to sponsor them financially so they could stay in school.)

The federal government supports all schools, both public and private. As a result, funding is so diluted that, for example, only elite secondary schools catering to the wealthy can avoid outrageous class sizes of up to 120 students.

Meanwhile, other challenges abound. 20,000 classrooms lack a teacher. There is a three-year waiting list for college, even for the few able to afford it. And, too often the graduates either find no work or flee abroad in search of better pay. (There are currently more Ghanaian-trained physicians in New York City than in all of Ghana. It's a crippling, ironic brain-drain.)

Nonetheless, Ghanaian children begin every morning with a song. And if they can—I told my American students afterward—so should we all.

* * *

I met Justice towards the end of my first week in Ghana. After five straight days of lectures, my colleagues and I had escaped the university to explore the nearby town of Cape Coast, and, with luck, finally immerse ourselves in the local culture. We'd had enough of imperial history and economic theory. We'd longed to roll up our sleeves and touch the real Africa, befriend real Ghanaians, instead of merely study about them.

Once we tumbled off the bus, however, we understood why our professors had kept us safely ensconced in a classroom for so long. Cape Coast was overwhelming. It wasn't just the press of people, the stark poverty, or the fetid open sewers. It was the onslaught of hawkers who descended upon us, marking us easy prey. Wouldn't we buy a bracelet? A painting? A wood carving? Or, after listening to some pathetic story, just hand over some money? Mostly teenaged boys, they pursued us down the street, tugging at our sleeves relentlessly. There seemed to be no escape. And, unfortunately, that moment foreshadowed most of our interactions with Ghanaians during our six-week stay. I guess I'd yet again been naïve to hope for anything else.

Then Justice appeared at my elbow. A skinny boy of fourteen, he proffered no wares, begged for no alms. He merely smiled pleasantly and asked in perfect English if there was anything in town he could show me. Deftly he guided me away from the crowds, pointing to various landmarks with pride. Soon he led me to a corner tucked behind the slave castle from where I could watch the fishermen land their boats then mend their nets. And all the while Justice talked avidly of his life, family, studies, even his dreams.

An hour later Justice delivered me back to the bus, handed me a large shell upon which he'd written his email, and asked only that I stay in touch. Immensely grateful, I pressed a 5000 Cedi note (about 50 cents) into his hand....

Two days later, the front desk clerk informed me when I'd returned to the hotel late one evening that a young man had spent the better part of the day waiting for me in the lobby. The clerk's elaborate frown tactfully expressed his displeasure.

When I headed down to the pool early the next morning, there was Justice again. I asked, "Why aren't you at school, Justice?" even though I already knew the answer. Most Ghanaian teens couldn't afford the fees required to continue beyond junior secondary school.

"The teacher sacked me," he replied.

Disappointed with this prologue to what I suspected to be a clever plea for money, I changed the subject. "Do you know how to swim?"

Justice was an apt pupil, doggedly splashing and dunking his head despite repeatedly choking on water. Afterward, I succumbed to his bait. "OK, Justice, why did your teacher sack you?"

"I lost my dictionary."

I waited for him to follow with a request for the price of a replacement. He never did. He just thanked me for his first swimming lesson.

I didn't believe Justice's story about the dictionary. Nonetheless, I marveled at his ability to read me so well, to provide the human connection I'd so longed for, while waiting for me to elicit his need for a donation. In the end I gave him the money, then reluctantly told him he could never return.

I couldn't forget Justice—his obvious intelligence, captivating charm, quiet determination, and cunning resourcefulness. As I began the next academic year, my new students seemed to take for granted everything that he'd longed for. I hoped to find within them a little of what so impressed me about him.

I spent that year, and every year since, searching for Justice.

✳ ✳ ✳

"Cape Coast Castle...stands outside the limits of time," wrote Ghanaian poet Kwadwo Opoku-Agyemang. "And the sea mourns under us, because it remembers the dead, and the widowed rivers that fed it."

Early one evening, I stared out at the placid, star-lit Gulf of Guinea, the full moon rising over it in silent majesty.

Nonetheless, I felt no peace. A scant hundred yards down the beach loomed Cape Coast Castle—massive, dark, brooding, the most infamous of seventy-six such slave castles marring an otherwise beautiful West African coast. Did the waves really remember? Did they grieve? Or were they pitiless, even oblivious?

Between 1653 and 1833—after which the British finally abolished slavery in its colonies—Cape Coast Castle imprisoned more than a thousand Africans at a time, some of the fifteen million people Africa eventually lost to slavery. They languished in unspeakable squalor for as long as six weeks in the castle before passing through the dreaded "Door of No Return" to the waiting ships, and the horror of the Middle Passage to America.

I'd endured only a few moments in one of the cavernous donjons, beholding the grisly scars where the desperate inmates had clawed with bloody fingers. Frankly, I couldn't even begin to imagine their torment, their despair.

How, then, could I ever hope to teach about it?

Some, like poet Opoku-Agyemang, would have me point an accusatory finger at "the predatory European society." Others retort defensively that the Africans were likewise to blame, since they themselves had engaged in slavery long before the European invasion. While true, this overlooks that Africans had originally practiced a far more benign slavery, where no one pretended slaves were mere chattel, no one brutalized or worked them to death. On the other hand, when, after abolition, West African emissary George Ferguson implored upland African chiefs to stop selling their brethren into chains, the chiefs murdered him. They, too, had been consumed with greed.

No, The Blame Game serves no one and nothing. A cursory review of world history reveals that all races have the blood of slavery and genocide on their hands. We're all guilty. And—given that anyone who denies the humanity of another corrupts his own as well—we're all victims, too.

The West Africans, who now guard the slave castles, have carved this wisdom on a stone monument: "This is in everlasting memory of our anguished ancestors. May those who died rest in peace. May those who return find their roots. May humanity never again perpetrate such injustices against humanity. We the living vow to uphold this."

The weighty oath haunted me that evening as I gazed at the waves crashing onto the rocks beneath Cape Coast Castle. And I realized that the sea, ever remorseless, neither remembers nor cares. It seeks only to wash all castles and all memory away into oblivion.

It is for teachers like me to, as best we can, beat back the waves of soothing forgetfulness; and, even more importantly, ennoble students to recognize slavery's kindred in modern assaults on human rights and dignity. (As many a seventy million souls continue to writhe in slavery today, some to acquire the raw materials for our smart phones.)

It's not an easy task, obviously; nor without its risks. As the poet lamented, "I have seen the slaver cross himself, and reason with faith in profit's favor." Indeed, the powerful today similarly disguise their greed as religious or patriotic crusades; and, like the upland chiefs, will target anyone who exposes them, who teaches of modern slavery, oppression, injustice—and our complicity.

For me, only one question has lingered after that moonlit, melancholy evening: Do I have the courage to truly honor the legacy of Cape Coast Castle? Do I dare follow in the intrepid, ill-fated footsteps of George Ferguson?

"And the sea cackled, and foamed at the mouth."

***

I followed with uncommon interest President Obama's visit to Ghana. I couldn't help but notice the striking fact that, in spite of all his praise for Ghana's fledgling democracy, Obama did not visit the monument to the country's first president and father of African democracy, Kwame Nkrumah.

In Ghana, I studied everything from its geography, history and economy to its religions, schools, and music. (My 7th grade history curriculum included Africa and the ancient empire of Ghana.) But it was Nkrumah's story—his dream, his triumph, and ultimately his failure— that captivated me then and continues to both inspire and trouble me today.

Kwame Nkrumah studied first at a Ghanaian Catholic seminary, then completed his formal education in the United States, earning a BA in Theology from Lincoln University, and later an MS in Education and an MA in Philosophy from the University of Pennsylvania.

Nonetheless, his heart remained in Africa. In 1945, he founded The West African National Secretariat with the goal of decolonizing Africa. He eventually led the movement to free Ghana from British rule, endured prison for his efforts, but emerged victorious in 1960 as the president of the first politically independent sub-Saharan African republic.

If only Nkrumah's story had ended there!

Political independence is one thing, economic independence quite another (and, as will become clear, one without the other is meaningless).

Ghana lacked industry and so had to import most of its manufactured goods. It earned foreign currency to do so by exporting its gold, bauxite, cocoa, and palm oil, with multinational corporations controlling the domestic mining/harvesting operations, and pocketing most of the profits. Thus, despite Ghana's wealth of natural resources, it remained poor and underdeveloped.

Nkrumah became obsessed with fostering Ghanaian industry. He'd need foreign loans and investment to do so, yet none of them came without manipulative strings and oppressive debt. (This is still the predicament of most "developing" nations today.)

Nkrumah's grand plan for the Akosombo Dam illustrates the dilemma poignantly. Nkrumah hoped the dam's generators, harnessing the largest reservoir on Earth, would enable Ghana to process the country's bauxite into aluminum, creating a huge new national industry and spawning many others. American industrial and World Bank financiers would not permit such independence, however. They'd provide funding for the project, but only if they controlled the smelters, only if Ghana used imported bauxite, and exported the aluminum for manufacture elsewhere. The financiers also insisted Ghana sell them most of the generated electricity at vastly deflated prices. Ghana's profit would be minimal. In order to repay the loans, the country would have to "tighten its belt": increase taxes, reduce public programs, silence trade unions.

What choice did Nkrumah have? Hoping the dam's electricity might one day fuel Ghana's own factories, he made the Faustian bargain. He vented his frustration by publishing his *Neo-Colonialism: The Last Stage of Imperialism*, and working fervently to create a Pan-African alliance of nations that, perhaps, could demand some measure of economic self-determination.

It was not to be. In 1966, with the complicity of the CIA, the Ghanaian military deposed Nkrumah. He died from cancer in exile five years later.

A long series of other often violent coups ensued, ending only in 1992 with a new constitution and the re-establishment of democratically elected governments—all of which have remained ever-so subservient to the International Monetary Fund and the World Bank, leaving Ghana saddled with spiraling foreign debt and crippling austerity measures.

During my studies there, it wrenched my soul to meet so many charming but hapless Ghanaian children such as Justice. He struggled so hard to stay in school. Yet, I knew that, if he graduated, he'd find few jobs requiring his hard-won knowledge and skills. Like his country, he'd likely remain forever frustrated, forever poor.

I wish Obama had visited Kwame Nkrumah's monument. There, in honor of Nkrumah's courageous vision for all Africa's children, he could have acknowledged how true freedom requires so much more than just a chance to vote. Instead, Obama heralded Ghana as a model of African democracy. "We must start with a simple premise that Africa's future is up to Africans," he said.

What a beguiling platitude—an insult to Nkrumah's memory; and, coming from the lips of a man with African roots, a galling betrayal.

ANTIGUA

West Indies

It's painful to admit I was as much at fault as the kids. But time has given me a new perspective on that long, miserable nightmare we shared on Antigua. While it remains the worst summer of my life, I am wiser for the experience. At least, I know I'd be a better group-leader if I were to do it again. Perhaps that is some consolation.

I had imagined the eleven high school students who accompanied me on the volunteer project in 1988 would be naïve, idealistic, intent on saving the world. My job would be to ease their disappointment when they realized they could barely make a difference in the small, local community. It was I, however, who would be disappointed.

I suspected something was wrong when I met the group. Hailing from the most affluent New England boarding schools, they tried to out-do each other with tales of their parents' wealth.

Anne was the worst: "Why just the other day, when I was heading for lunch at Daddy's club as usual, my Beemer had a flat. Oh, it was an absolutely horrid day!"

Horrid? But things only got worse.

Two days later, I brought Anne to her morning volunteer project. She'd be working with kids at the hospital.

"But, Dave," she whispered, her lip quivering, "they're sick!"

"That's the idea, Anne," I responded impatiently. "These kids came here for long-term treatment. Many are far from home, and they're all lonely, scared, and bored. Just play with them or read to them. Help them forget their sickness. They'll soon fall in love with you, Anne, and you with them. Trust me."

A few minutes later, though, when Anne spied one young boy who had been severely burned, her eyes rolled up in her head, and she fainted dramatically. The actor in me was impressed with the performance, but the project leader was growing exasperated.

Most of the other "volunteers" were no better. That evening, for instance, Gerald announced haughtily that he wouldn't even consider eating the "vile" dinner one of the others had created. When it was Kimberly's turn to clean the bathroom, she refused, explaining, "I don't do bathrooms." Jonathan merely complained: "Why didn't they tell me the island was full of Blacks?" Frankly, the only thing they were really interested in was either going to the beach, or necking out back.

Unfortunately, I did little to disguise my disgust. The group responded in kind, becoming even more obnoxious. When we finally left, I'm sure the whole island breathed a sigh of relief.

My final journal entry said it all: "I have infinite patience for disadvantaged kids. I have none for these spoiled, selfish snobs. Good riddance!"

Today I read that with chagrin. For now I realize that wealthy students can be just a needy as poor ones, albeit in different, sometimes ugly ways. They, too, require patience and understanding. If only I had known that in Antigua, I might have enabled those kids to learn so much about the world and about themselves. But I didn't. And that's why I failed.

I hope only that, although Anne, for instance, surely has no fond memories of me, she does cherish a few of that small, burned boy, to whom she finally did read some stories.

THE SEA OF CORTEZ

Mexico

I paddled my kayak warily through the silent cove, just off Danzante Island. After all, it was after 9 p.m. on a moonless night. I could see nothing save the starry heavens above, and what I believed to be their undulating reflection around me. But when I reached overboard to trail my hand casually in the cool water, I gasped; for the pinpricks of light coalesced around my hand and glowed brilliantly, as if I'd just placed it into some sort of liquid Plutonium.

This was bioluminescence, the sun's energy stored in plankton, catalyzed by my disturbing the water. I'd heard of it, but never actually seen it. Giddy, I splashed crazily, illuminating the water all around my kayak. Amazing!

Thus, my spring vacation kayaking in Mexico's Sea of Cortez turned out to be a week-long voyage of discovery. For example, I learned the islands are the vestiges of ancient volcanoes; and the sea itself occupies a valley left when the huge Baja Peninsula slid, earthquake by earthquake, inexorably towards the northwest. One day, it, too, will be an island.

Every afternoon after a morning's paddle to a new campsite, I snorkeled in water too cold for my comfort, but abundant nonetheless with tropical fish: yellow-striped Sergeant Majors, sparkling blue Damsel Fish, even some menacing Moray Eels. My favorite, though, were the hermaphroditic Rainbow Wrasse. On the beach afterward, I gleaned from a dog-eared, waterlogged nature book that they're born female; then, at least one in each school eventually transforms into a male. Who decides which one? Fascinating!

Above the islands soared numerous birds, such as the stern Pelicans, the adorable Grebes, and the crafty Cormorants. The pterodactyl-looking Frigate Birds, with their odd, forked tails, were my favorite. Unlike the others, they couldn't dive beneath the water for fish, and so often made do with stealing what they could.

Everyone on the trip agreed that the Blue-Footed Boobies had the best name.

After dinner each evening, my twelve companions—hailing from as far away as New Zealand—and I traded silly stories, learned quickly to avoid politics, and read from Steinbeck's *Log from the Sea of Cortez*. Sometimes poignant, often hilarious, the book harkened back to different times, a forgotten Mexico, but universal and enduring themes.

Once the light faded, we studied the constellations with binoculars. By the second night, I could readily locate both the Orion Nebula and the Pleiades Sisters.

Afterward, despite the hard ground, sleep was easy—the just reward after twenty miles of paddling a day through ten-foot swells against forty-mile-an-hour winds. (OK, I'm exaggerating a bit....) Each day, though, my shoulders ached less as I grew in strength and skill. Soon I could even climb back into a kayak without capsizing.

Yes, I had an exciting adventure for a vacation. What I really did, though, was study: Biology, Astronomy, Natural and Human History, Physical Education, Literature...and even how to thrive in a small, diverse, mutually-dependent community of novice kayakers. I learned a lot—inadvertently, gleefully.

All too soon, I found myself back in Union City, safely ensconced in Room B14, in front of 33 teenagers who slouched in tiny desks arranged in tidy rows, with windows too small and high to see outside. And I endeavored to teach the kids about the world and themselves.

When they squirmed with impatience or boredom, I no longer wondered what was the matter.

GUATEMALA AND HONDURAS

Central America

Eighteen Rabbit died at the hands of his nephew, Sky Monster. He was the best known and most powerful Mayan ruler. The 13th god/king of the Copán dynasty, 18 Rabbit ruled well for 43 years until his violent death—a passing that presaged the collapse of not only Copán (located in modern Honduras), but virtually all the Mayan civilizations of the Classic Period.

Eschewing his father's wars of conquest that had left Copán in a precarious state, Eighteen Rabbit oversaw a renaissance of Mayan art and architecture. His many projects included Copán's Great Plaza, the unequaled Hieroglyphic Staircase (containing 1,200 inscriptions, the longest known Mayan text), Copán's magnificent Temple 22, and 7 elaborately detailed *estelas* (tall, stone monuments) depicting himself as various Mayan gods.

But even Eighteen Rabbit's enlightened vision could not prevent Copán's demise, the inexorable result of the city-state's own success. Once Copán's population reached a pinnacle of perhaps 27,000 inhabitants, the country-side could no longer provide enough food. Massive deforestation—for agriculture and for fuel (voracious limestone kilns provided plaster for Copán's extensive monuments)—caused soil depletion, erosion, and may have even contributed to a devastating drought. The incipient disaster led to social upheaval and political unrest as well, which may explain why Sky Monster decided to murder his uncle, Eighteen Rabbit.

Sky Monster lorded over neighboring Quirigua (pronounced key-ree-GUA), a smaller Mayan city to the north (in modern Guatemala), which was in thrall to Copán. In fact, Sky Monster ruled only at the behest of Eighteen Rabbit.

Evidently an ingrate, Sky Monster may have decided he no longer wanted to pay his uncle tribute. After all, Quirigua faced the same starvation as Copán. For whatever reason, he captured Eighteen Rabbit and brought him back to Quirigua for execution.

Perhaps to show his uncle the dignity of a noble death, or perhaps to magnify himself, Sky Monster first challenged Eighteen Rabbit to a ceremonial ball game, the loser to be sacrificed. Of course, being decades younger, he easily defeated Eighteen Rabbit. He then threw him down a giant set of stone stairs and beheaded him.

One summer, I stood before the huge, 1,400-year-old carved stone tablet depicting Eighteen Rabbit's inglorious demise, possibly on the very spot where had it occurred. It lay at the base of the stairs, Sky Monster's own *estela* towering in triumph above it.

Six other estelas adorn the surrounding plaza—the most exquisite in all Mesoamerica, the largest standing 36 feet high and weighing an astonishing 66 tons. They are the quite compelling political propaganda of a desperate man, and a doomed civilization.

I learned all this while on a ten-day excursion through Central America. I'd wanted to spend time with my aunt and uncle, who'd already booked tickets for the tour. But, frankly, I dreaded the prospect of being cooped up on a bus with 42 other gringos, speaking little if any Spanish.

Fortunately, our attentive Guatemalan tour guide provided us the equivalent of a hands-on, graduate-level course in Guatemala—not only its glorious Mayan heritage, varied geography, abundant and beautiful flora and fauna, but the inevitability, complexity, and tragedy of the recent civil war as well, including even the United States' shameful complicity.

I remembered again my love of travel, history, and learning; and how much I enjoy sharing that love every year with my new students.

THE COPPER CANYONS

Mexico

I spent my spring break crossing off one item from my long bucket list: taking the train through and hiking around Mexico's breathtaking Copper Canyons. I had a wonderful but disturbing time.

The final few days I stayed at a rustic hotel nestled in a pine valley amid Native Mexican (Tarahumara) homes. The Sierra Lodge had no electricity, but provided lanterns and a fireplace in each room, which the employees kindled while I was having dinner in the lodge's huge dining room. The meal was usually preceded by a happy hour with free Margarita's for all, but I declined. You see, I was the hotel's only guest.

The same was true nearly everywhere I went during my 9-day trip. It was the off season. The real explanation had to do with rampant fears about Mexico's violent drug wars. The locals lamented how tourism had declined by nearly 80 percent.

During my sumptuous but lonely dinners by lantern-light at The Lodge, I mused quite a bit about the whole depressing situation. Not only were other travelers not enjoying one of the world's great wonders, but thousands of those employed in tourism were losing their livelihood. What would they do? Many, desperate, would undoubtedly head for the United States border. After all, picking strawberries and grapes is better than starving.

Thus, the drug wars will come full circle. We in America use by far more illicit drugs than any other nation on Earth. We provide not only a robust demand for the drugs fueling the Mexican wars, but an apparently free market for high powered weapons as well. Our hands are certainly not innocent or bloodless with regard to the Mexican violence, nor with the resulting unemployment and increased pressure on our borders.

How could we decrease the demand for drugs here? Our "War on Drugs" has proved to be no more successful than our other wars. Perhaps we should focus instead on prevention, such as investing in inner-city communities. (Although suburban ones use no fewer drugs.) We could bring supermarkets and jobs back, refurbish the schools, send our best teachers there.

Of course, all that would require funds—which, unfortunately, we're currently squandering abroad at a rate of about $1 million per soldier per year; trillions so far. Perhaps we could reevaluate our nation's priorities?

Amazing how a plummet in Mexican tourism can lead to a discussion of all sorts of seeming unrelated topics.

Which is my real point: Our world is, indeed, a tightly-knit tapestry, every thread interconnected. All of our decisions, both as individuals and as a nation, have (to mix my metaphors) consequences rippling out in all directions, eventually coming back home to us.

Why don't we emphasize that truism well in our schools, the notion of personal responsibility, of thinking globally but acting locally? (Maybe because it doesn't appear on high stakes tests.) A hamburger here may destroy part of a Brazilian rainforest. A long shower in the morning can endanger wildlife in the Sacramento Delta. The funds for another flat-screen TV could also build a well in Africa, saving hundreds of lives, most of them children's.

And a decision to experiment with drugs will harm not only oneself, but communities as far away as Mexico's Copper Canyons.

✳ ✳ ✳

Satevó is a tiny village at the bottom of the Copper Canyons. It rests more than 7,000 feet below the Sierra Madre towering above, and four jarring, white-knuckle hours from the nearest paved road.

Satevó hides a gem, the "lost" Church of San Miguel, all that remains of the mission that Jesuits established there in the early 1600s (a contemporary to Virginia's Jamestown). But why would they build such a cathedral-like structure—with three domes and a three-tiered bell tower—in such a small, far-flung Native village? Alas, the records disappeared. Nobody knows.

Clearly, though, the Jesuits were intent on replacing the Natives' culture with their own.

Today, adjacent to the lovely church stands a far more humble, but equally lost school where two forgotten teachers continue the Jesuits' mission.

One of them, Manuel came running toward me after I'd snapped a photo of the school. Once he learned I was a fellow educator who spoke Spanish, he persuaded me to let him guide me around the church, the village, and the school.

Manuel brought with him on his tour some sort of teacher-training manual about various educational theories, most of which I'd never heard of. He clung to it as a sacred text, gushing with enthusiasm. "Oh God, a newbie," I thought to myself. But who else would be stationed in such a difficult, isolated school outpost? (The same is true in inner cities in the U.S., where too-often our least-qualified teachers do their best against all odds.)

Manuel was personable, earnest, and passionate. I liked him.

He also was desperately lonely. "Everyone in this village laughs at me," he complained. "I'm so educated and practice Buddhism, chanting when I meditate. They just think I'm weird. Whom can I talk to?"

I asked about his colleague, but Manuel didn't answer.

The next day, I hiked back to Satevó to visit Manuel's classroom of 12 first, second, and third-graders. There was no theory evident. Manuel struggled just to get all the children to sit down (and I recalled my first classroom in Spain). He greeted me warmly, but then complained in front of the class about an incorrigible boy in the back of the room, José, who, when he showed up, made class instruction nearly impossible.

"Why don't I tutor him," I offered quickly. "Then you can focus on the rest of the class?"

I sat down next to José, an adorably cute Native boy, and began to guide him though the two-digit subtraction problem Manuel had written on the whiteboard in barely decipherable light brown marker. I started by pointing out how we'd have to borrow from the tens place in order to subtract the ones, but poor José seemed baffled. I soon realized he didn't understand place value at all. Nor subtraction. In fact, he could only barely write the numbers, so that's where I focused our lesson. "Try to make the top and the bottom of each number touch the blue lines," I urged him.

And he tried. Despite everything, he did want to learn. Oh, I liked José, too!

Meanwhile, Manuel kept sneaking over to eavesdrop on my tutoring, convinced, I suspect, that I was implementing some incredibly progressive American pedagogy.

I met Manuel's colleague, Teresa, during the lunch of warm milk over puffed wheat cereal and a bean burrito—the only meal of the day for many of the students. Teresa shunned both of us, though.

"And why wouldn't she?" I mused afterward on the four-mile trek back to my hotel. Teresa taught grades four through six, and faced the challenge of teaching Manuel's students after he'd failed to.

I felt tremendous compassion for Teresa, for Manuel, and for José. They were all doing the best they could, in a little school in a small village, next to a beautiful church, lost in an immense canyon few have ever heard of.

THE HIMALAYAS

Nepal

I stood outside the lovely Buddhist monastery of Upper Pisang, Nepal, beheld the village of Lower Pisang below, and sighed ruefully.

The two young monks in traditional burgundy-red robes to my left, had they read my thoughts, might have reminded me that all suffering begins with clinging, that nothing lasts forever. I mourned, if not the loss of the legendary Himalayan Annapurna Circuit, at least its swift and radical transformation.

The Annapurna Circuit winds for about 150 miles around a Nepalese mountain range of the same name. Beginning in lush, tropical lowlands, the challenging trail follows a thundering river, eventually leading up over Thorong-La Pass at 17,769 feet (the highest I'll ever likely hike). On the other side, another river plunges back down to the lowlands again. Boasting unparalleled views of quant villages, towering waterfalls and, of course, Himalayan peaks, the Annapurna Circuit has been a favorite for international trekkers for years.

And therein lies the problem. Trekkers like me are loving the Circuit to death. Over 70,000 of them visited last year. As a result, tourism, not agriculture, now dominates the local economy. And every village no matter how small (and small villages won't remain so for long.) is frantically replacing traditional homes with western-style trekking lodges.

That included Lower Pisang below me. I observed how one colorful new lodge crowded the next, their first-floor shops hawking souvenirs and fake Chinese-made North Face trekking gear. I wondered what the village had once looked like; but noted as well that the profits from those lodges had rebuilt the beautiful monastery and temple here in Upper

Pisang, from where the monks and I now gazed. There's a new school, too.

Nepal desperately needs the foreign capital and employment such tourism provides. But, is the money worth the terrible cost in culture?

And to the environment? A new dirt road replacing the Annapurna Trail will soon reach all the villages on either side of Thorong-La Pass. (Although, with the constant landslides, the road may never truly be finished—or safe.) The construction provides employment for hundreds of local peasants. But, with its erosion, it permanently scars a once pristine Shangri La.

Will the road and the development it brings help the trekking industry, or destroy it?

I glanced up from the village towards the Annapurna Peaks, which were supposedly arrayed majestically above, but remained maddeningly hidden. My few fellow trekkers and I had exchanged autumn crowds for summer monsoons—a gamble we eventually lost since, except for one, small, fleeting break in the clouds two days later, my friends and I never saw the mighty Himalayas.

The Annapurna Circuit is truly a remarkable, unforgettable place. I discovered so much beauty there, but so many gambles, dilemmas, trade-offs, and compromises as well.

Life, with its inevitable onrush of change, offers few easy decisions, even fewer right answers; and, as the monks might murmur, little at all to those who would cling to what was, no matter how wonderful and simple it might have seemed.

Such is the complicated, messy world education ought to prepare students to inhabit, and perhaps even to lead. We Americans, however, still teach our children to guess between A, B, C, or D.

One can see very far, indeed, from Upper Pisang, Manang Province, along Nepal's famed Annapurna Circuit.

THE ANDES

Peru

As I trudged down from Dead Woman's Pass, I'd had my doubts. My highest point along Peru's famed Inca Trail hadn't been as glorious as I'd imagined. In fact, the frigid rain and driving hail there had all but chased my two friends, guide, eight porters and me away; as if, like the Inca, themselves, I'd been cursed. Would the weather spoil this trip, too, just as it had my trek through Nepal the summer before?

Inti, the Inca sun god, smiled the next day, though, revealing a trail that surpassed all my dreams. Snow-covered peaks crowned the horizon as we made our way along a razorback ridge, with clouds and mists traversing the valleys below.

We camped that evening on a small plateau at the end of the ridge, and gaped at truly breath-taking vistas in all directions, even the back side of Machu Picchu Mountain.

Late that afternoon, William, our Peruvian guide, brought us to Phuyupatamarka, an impressive heart-shaped Inca ruin just below our campsite, notable for its cascading row of spring-fed fountains. "I want to share something really important with you today, essential before we finally arrive at our goal tomorrow, the citadel of Machu Picchu. You must understand Inca cosmology, codified, of course, by Pachacuti.

The amazing Pachacuti: ninth and greatest by far of the Inca lords, the visionary who'd not only expanded Cusco from a backwater hamlet into the largest empire of the 13th century—extending 2,400 miles along the Andes, embracing nearly 12 million diverse peoples, resplendent with architectural marvels that still inspire awe today—but who'd made of it a utopia where no one knew hunger.

"Pachacuti sought to discover and establish order in the universe," William explained drawing a chart in the dirt with the tip of his walking stick. "He divided his cosmology, as he did his empire, into four quadrants.

"The bottom left quadrant, for example, describes the trilogy of creation: the condor rules the heavens, the panther the Earth, and the serpent the underworld." (Pachacuti rebuilt his capital, Cusco, into the shape of a panther.) "The bottom right quadrant contains the trilogy of ethics: Don't steal. Don't lie. And don't be lazy. "I try to live up to them," William added somberly.

So, perhaps something more than ruins endures of Pachacuti and his grand Inca Empire.

Alas, as with all empires, it was oh-so fleeting. Pachacuti had prophesied some terrifying menace, and had created elaborate defenses along all roads leading back to Cusco. But he could never have foreseen Smallpox, the conquering Spaniards' greatest weapon. And, mercifully, he could never have imagined the ruthless cruelty with which the Spaniards would plunder then destroy all he had created, long before it had reached its ascendancy.

Thus, when I finally passed through the Sun Gate the next afternoon, and gasped as I beheld the remnants of the magnificent Machu Picchu arrayed below, one of the new Seven Wonders of the World, I was filled with awe and gratitude, but with sadness, too.

I know these emotions well, the constant companions, it seems to me, of anyone who dares to travel with an open mind and heart through the world, through history, and through life.

NEUWSCHWANSTEIN CASTLE

Füssen, Germany

I began this book with the mystical moment I shared with a gull just as I embarked on my first and most important adventure.

There was another such moment about three weeks later which I've kept secret all these years—perhaps because I feared it was just too personal, too presumptuous, too religious for someone who had become an avowed agnostic; or maybe it was just too overwhelming. Truly, I'm embarrassed to finally share it now.

Some background: I have always suffered from a pathologically low self-image. It's manifested in my stuttering, my 4th grade belief that I was destined for Hell, in my inability to graciously accept praise, my perpetual slouch that has done irreparable damage to my back and shoulders; and sometimes even, as a counselor once pointed out, in subconscious self-sabotage so that I could beat myself up afterward.

I once shared with that counselor, "The truth is, I'm inadequate in every aspect of my life." My claim hung in the air for a long moment, and then I burst out with cathartic laughter, "Well, that's ridiculous!" Still, it had long been my insidious, core belief.

"David," that counselor replied, "you need to let go of your perfectionism. You seem to believe you must be great or you're a failure. You're human, and thus imperfect, but still wonderful!" And then he added, echoing what many of my family, friends and colleagues had often expressed with befuddled frustration, "I just wish you could see yourself as we see you."

I'll never know how or why, in 1981, I overrode my self-doubt enough to undertake a pilgrimage abroad. Three weeks into a whirlwind tour of Europe before my studies in Spain, I visited Germany's fantastical Neuschwanstein Castle.

There was a long line to get inside. I'd always hated museums anyway, so, in spite of a dreary drizzle, I set off instead on a hike up the hills overlooking the castle hoping to take a stunning, poster-worthy photograph.

I followed a precarious trail. "I probably shouldn't do this alone," I muttered, but continued. Up and up I went, long after I'd taken my photo, impelled by some need to reach the summit. I glanced at my watch and realized I'd miss the final train back to Munich. Oh well. I trudged on.

I finally reached the crest and glimpsed in the distance a towering range of snow-capped mountains. I stood transfixed. Who'd have thought I'd ever see such beauty for myself? Who'd have thought I'd ever wander like this by myself?

At just that moment, a shaft of sun burst through the dark clouds and shone in my face. I whispered, "Behold, this is my beloved son, in whom I am well-pleased." (Matthew 3:17)

And I began to cry.

I have both suppressed and savored that memory ever since. I've dismissed it as just the silly imagining of an earnest, naive young man. And yet, every now and then, I've allowed myself to recall it, and feel good.

I realize now that, whether the biblical words came from God or the depth of my soul (is there a difference?), they were real, a truth I needed to hear; one everyone has been trying to tell me in their own way over the years, but I wouldn't, couldn't accept.

I read recently about the power of crafting, then reciting short affirmations. I created one for myself, a magical incantation of sorts that helps me ward off the specters of perfectionism and self-depreciation: "I am gifted, I am flawed, I am human: the perfect me." (David 3:15)

I wish this tortuous journey hadn't taken me so long. But maybe, as my Mom might explain, that's why God gave me all this borrowed time.

SANTANDER

Spain

Sally's postcard arrived like a love-letter—not just from her, but from the city she'd been visiting: Santander.

Santander! That beautiful town on the northern coast of Spain where Fate had brought me after college, city of laughing sea and stoic mountains, winter rains and summer mirth, desperate loneliness and oh-so-kind welcome.

Santander! How the memories came tumbling back, like so many disparate, long-forgotten pieces to a beloved puzzle I'd never managed to put together.

First, I recalled the *Farol*, the lighthouse out beyond the city, from where, forlorn and near despair, I'd braved the winds, stared out at the whitecaps, and strove to think great thoughts. (I'd majored in The Great Books, and so fancied myself a philosopher...)

Then, I remembered the sierra, Los Picos de Europa. On my first backpacking trip there, I'd rested outside a shepherd's hut, spellbound while early evening clouds crept silently over the pass, then down into the canyon, already dark below. Oh, I'd left Ohio far behind!

Wisps of faces and conversations came back, too. My Spanish friends had despised Americans—at least the idea of them—but had sheltered and tutored me patiently. They'd spoken proudly of having fended off both the Romans and the Moors, only to finally succumb more recently to that fascist, Franco. With whimsical bitterness they pointed to a cannon Franco had used to pound the city into submission now standing as an ironic monument, still aimed at the town center.

Santander had taught me history wasn't just a captivating story.

Oh, to return to the small mom and pop *carnicerías*, *panaderías*, and *ferreterías* where I'd shopped for meat, bread, and sundries! I'd never escaped without some conversation with the owners, the other shoppers hushing at the sound of my "*yanqui*" accent, eager to collect juicy gossip for the neighborhood, but nodding in smiling approval as my Spanish improved week by week. "*Claro, es maestro,*" they'd murmured. "Of course, he's a teacher." (They'd revered educators in Spain.)

Yes, it was in Santander that I'd unwittingly begun what became my vocation. I'd taught English at various schools throughout the city, armed with nothing more than my diploma, a contagious enthusiasm, an easy laugh, and a willingness to work hard. It was enough. (It still is.)

All those dear recollections from one silly post card! Ah, but Santander had been an adventure, after all; one where I'd learned self-confidence, accepted humility, fell in love with teaching, and, above all, felt my first real, conscious joy at the simple, profound act of living. Santander made me who I am today.

If I finally have any true, great thought, Sally's post card from Santander enabled me to assemble it from so many jigsaw memories, and it is this: Adventure—taking risks, traveling either literally or figuratively, feeling lost, depending on new friends, and finding one's way back home again changed forever—this is one of the great purposes of life, whether you're rambling on borrowed time or not.

And the only education that matters is not one that raises test scores or promises an ever-elusive financial security. No, real education prepares us, then inspires us to undertake that life-long adventure—to Santander, or wherever.

Ellison

SPREAD THE WORD!

Did you enjoy *Santander*?

Please tell your friends about it, perhaps even post a link to its Amazon page on social media. You can like its Facebook page, *Santander, a memoir*. Also, consider writing a short (or not) review on Amazon.

Thank you for reading my book.   DE

Ellison

ACKNOWLEDGEMENT

I thank David Nieskens, my first mentor teacher, who planted the outrageous idea of writing a column one day; Jack Lyness, former editor of *The Argus*, who took a chance on the mousy character who showed up a day late for his interview; and my partner, Edgar Antonio, who chose the book's title and designed its cover.

Above all, I must acknowledge Corinna Dooha-Chambers, who, after adopting me as an honorary uncle, became my editor and cheerleader.

Ellison

ELLISON'S OTHER BOOKS

Bloodletting: Why Education Reform is Killing America's Schools

Bloodletting - an uncompromising, provocative exposé about education reform in the United States.

Ellison provides an evidenced-based overview of the on-going fiasco of American education, using cogent, accessible language, often citing his own poignant and too-often heart-wrenching personal experience. *Bloodletting* is a bold treatise from a 36-year veteran educator and a passionate writer.

Chalk Dust: A Teacher's Marks

Chalk Dust - a mini-masterpiece of the teaching life.

This collection of over 70 of Ellison's best columns (many of which reappear in *Santander*) is at once touching, delightful, poignant, and unflinchingly honest. *Chalk Dust* delivers fresh, informed, and multifaceted views of education by a teacher/administrator who has worked in the trenches and loves what he does.

Printed in Great Britain
by Amazon